SHARP CORNERS:
URBAN OPERATIONS AT CENTURY'S END

Roger J. Spiller

U.S. Army Command and General Staff College Press
Fort Leavenworth, Kansas

Published by Books Express Publishing
Copyright © Books Express, 2012
ISBN 978-1-78039-672-9

Books Express publications are available from all good retail and online booksellers. For publishing proposals and direct ordering please contact us at: info@books-express.com

Contents

Introduction v
Part One. On Urban Operations and the Urban Environment.............1
Part Two. Under Fire: Urban Operations in Perspective 37
Part Three. Metropolis, or Modern Urban Warfare 85
Part Four. Theory to Practice: Implications for DTLOMS..............123
Appendix. Catalog of Selected Urban Battles................................133
Select Bibliography 139

Introduction

This study was directed by the Commanding General, US Army Training and Doctrine Command, in the summer of 1999. NATO operations against Yugoslavia had just begun. Notwithstanding official announcements that ground forces would not be needed for the time being, expectations ran high that ground troops would ultimately have to be employed. The precise nature of the operations they would be called on to perform could not be foreseen, and consequently neither the size nor the precise character of the forces to be committed could be decided at the time. The range of possibilities was enough to give any commander or operational planner headaches: American ground forces could be engaged in direct combat within or beyond the province of Kosovo, then the focal point of NATO operations, against conventional forces or their surrogates. US troops could also be employed as an element of a peacekeeping operation confined to the province itself, or perhaps beyond, or any gradation of commitment between these extremes. No one with official responsibility could envision a scenario without ground troops of any sort.

Only one assumption could be made with any sort of confidence: once ground forces were introduced, a significant part of their duties would be performed not in the open countryside but in areas that could to some degree be characterized as urban. Some such areas might be very small, no more than a village perhaps, with a population numbering in the tens. Some might be towns with only a few thousand inhabitants. Others might be much larger municipalities, with populations running to the tens of thousands. The question naturally arose: to what degree was the US Army prepared for this mission, ill-defined as it was at that particular time?

Some of these questions have since been answered. NATO's air campaign forced the Yugoslavian Army from Kosovo and opened the way for the deployment of a multinational force to reestablish civic order in that province. NATO ground forces have not been challenged seriously so far. But Kosovo is hardly peaceful. Hatreds, both ancient and recent, threaten the stability of the region for the foreseeable future. It is likely that many of Kosovo's problems will be played out in the villages, towns, and cities of the province, but no one knows how or when these will be resolved. History is yet to have its say.

The deployment of ground forces into Kosovo is only the latest in an ever-growing list of contingency operations conducted by the United

States and other leading nations in recent years. Some commentators have made the dubious claim that this kind of undertaking has become more frequent since the end of the Cold War, but it is more probable that the overriding burdens of the Cold War obscured what was under those circumstances a minor class of military operation. Contingency operations then made a smaller claim on the public's attention, even while they kept America's armed forces gainfully employed. The record shows that the United States conducted more than 250 contingency operations around the world between 1945 and 1976, not including the Korean and Vietnam Wars. In 40 percent of these operations, the US commitment took the form of ground forces, usually in less than division strength. More to the point of this study, however, most of those operations were conducted in urban areas.

So, an argument could easily be made that US armed forces, and the Army in particular, have a considerable body of experience in conducting limited operations in urban areas, some of it very recent indeed. Of the most important American operations since the end of the Vietnam War—Grenada, Beirut, Panama, the Persian Gulf War, Bosnia-Herzegovina, Haiti, Somalia, and now Kosovo—only the Gulf War could be said to have been carried out beyond the confines of an urban area, and even in this case, Kuwait City and the bombing of Baghdad were an important element of the larger campaign.

A collection of operational experiences does not, by itself, guarantee that an army will learn from them, and this returns us to the question of the Army's readiness to undertake the urban missions of the future. These experiences, as well as the experiences of other armies, have contributed to an impressively large body of professional military literature. This literature includes historical case studies, technical and topical studies, studies on the employment of specific weapons and weapons systems, and the tactics to be employed by particular branches both singly and in combination with one another. A comprehensive bibliography of these materials would be several inches thick. If only weight and utility were synonymous.

Such a compilation would contain the US Army's own Field Manual 90-10, *Military Operations in Urbanized Terrain,* last issued in 1979. When I began this study, a revision of FM 90-10 was already under way. The Joint Chiefs of Staff had assigned joint doctrinal proponency for urban operations to the Marine Corps, whose task was to formulate a doctrinal concept that would form the basis for a new Joint manual, for which the Army would serve as the technical review authority. By no means, then, should the present study be seen as the Army's main effort at coming to terms with the contemporary shape of urban operations.

Given the great variety and scope of these initiatives within and beyond the Army, and the body of knowledge that has been created already, one might well ask why this study is required? What could be left to study?

The answer to these questions lies partly in the guidance for this study. First of all, the intended audience for this paper is the Army as a whole. To a certain degree, the subject of urban warfare has come to be seen, justly or not, as an unwelcome distraction from the real business of an army, a relatively minor class of military problem that can be solved best by the application of time-honored tactical principles or by means of technological superiority. This view implies that not the whole Army, but only certain parts of it, need consider the unique challenges of modern urban conflict in its many forms. Under the circumstances, this approach hardly prepares the Army as a whole for the demands of a military future that promises a continuation of the trend towards urban operations witnessed in the immediate past. Ignoring these demands, or relegating them to small cadres of specialists, is not a viable course of action.

So, first of all, this paper aims at reviving interest in urban conflict and restoring the subject to the place it deserves in any modern army, and most particularly our own.

Another, equally important aspect of the guidance was that this investigation should address the challenge of what has come to be called, rather misleadingly, "the asymmetric threat," by which term is meant adversaries whose capabilities cannot hope to mimic our own. These antagonists harbor intentions and define their successes in ways that differ significantly from those of orthodox armed forces whose strategic and operational values derive from long traditions. The challenge thus posed to modern armed forces has not been adequately addressed.

Behind this guidance lies the suspicion that weaker adversaries in the future would choose as their *preferred* battleground the vast urban agglomerations of the world. In writings on historical and contemporary urban operations, one often sees that armies have long had an aversion to operating in the urban environment. This is an old and well-founded tradition. Unconventional adversaries often have been able to capitalize upon this aversion, but it is by no means certain that the advantage is constantly on their side. No fighting force is ever permitted to indulge its operational preferences with impunity. War and lesser forms of conflict do not organize themselves for anyone's benefit.

We know that in times past, armies have been defeated as much by their own shortcomings as by the actions of their enemies. These armies were so reluctant to make critical changes in their time-honored habits that they offered their enemies a vulnerability to exploit. A disjuncture between the habits of modern armies and those of their less conventional adversaries may be growing wider, creating a gap so wide that it cannot be bridged even by the most heroic ingenuity. The ability and willingness to envision and then to enact new ways of fighting may be the most dangerous asymmetry of all in the world of modern conflict.

Modern professional soldiers have learned by long and hard trial that war can no longer be thought of merely as an event, fought out without reference to its larger context. The concept of war as a strategic phenomenon with discernible parts we now call campaigns is well fixed in professional military literature. Since the emergence of the operational art in the early 1980s, the US Army's doctrines, tactics, techniques, and procedures have been attuned to this broader conception of war. But, we know, the Army's most recent thinking on urban conflict is represented by an ancient field manual, outdating by several years the principles by which we now conceive, plan, and guide our current operations. The question of how, precisely, urban conflict fits within the operational art is a question still waiting for an answer, and one, it is hoped, to which this study will contribute.

Like Gaul, the study is made of three parts.

The first part is based on the assumption that in order to take a city apart one must first know how to put it together. A substantial literature on urban design, planning, and management has never been exploited in a study of urban warfare, though a flash of common sense would tell us that these subjects are highly interrelated.

The second part attempts to place urban warfare into some perspective. No end of confusion has arisen over the years because of a failure to distinguish what is truly new from what is merely unfamiliar. Aspects of urban life, design, and urban fighting, thought by some observers to be precedent shattering, most often turn out to have been several hundred, if not thousands, of years old. If nothing else, simply knowing that others have faced the same problem has a calming effect, but when those others have found a solution, then the effect is educational.

The last part of this study attempts to fuse what has been discussed in the first two parts and suggests how we might make a fresh start at understanding a very difficult form of war in the future. That there are urban operations, perhaps outright urban war in our future, there is no doubt. The only question is when, and what can we do about it now?

        Roger J. Spiller
        George C. Marshall Professor of Military History

        Fort Leavenworth, Kansas
        June 2000

No operational imagination required. A Sarajevo neighborhood, 1998

Official photo courtesy Dr. Richard Swain

Part One

On Urban Operations and the Urban Environment

Defining Urban Operations

This study investigates the nature and conduct of modern urban operations. As a distinct type of military action, urban operations may well be the most influential form of conflict in the future. For some, urban operations are already the preferred form of military action. Others are very likely to discover the advantages of operating in this particular way in the future. If these trends continue, it means that the conduct of modern war is about to turn a sharp corner, away from its customary forms, toward different, less well-understood modes of action. If experience is any guide, this turning will not be dramatic; it will be composed of a thousand minor events, accruing so gradually that it evades notice. The sharp corners will be clear only in retrospect. For the moment, therefore, the question becomes: what can be known now about this mode of operation, and how should that knowledge affect our thinking?

It is significant that no generally agreed upon definition yet exists for these sorts of operation. Here, urban operations are considered broadly; they are all those military operations involving an urban environment.[1] This working definition is used in order to examine how the urban environment influences the conduct of military operations in general, as well as to consider this particular kind of military operation from a longer perspective. A longer perspective is needed just now, when military professionals everywhere are beginning to think seriously about urban operations for the first time in several years, and when armies are making new calculations about the rightful place that urban operations should occupy in the larger world of defense strategies.

As with any complex subject, first encounters with urban operations are likely to be confusing. A kind of vacuum surrounds the subject. No body of military theory directly addresses this kind of operation. Military doctrines are long out of date. Studies of urban battles generally do not address city fighting in a way that would be useful to a military professional who is trying to understand what makes this form of war unique. Under the circumstances, opinion holds court unencumbered by fact. The unfamiliar is often mistaken for something new, even though very little about urban operations is new at all.

But urban operations *seem* new. In fact, today's resurgence of interest is attributed to reasons that would not have sounded new even twenty years ago, namely:

- The performance of conventional forces in recent urban operations.
- A perceived increase in the frequency of such operations.
- A perceived imbalance between the national cost and national benefit of such operations.
- The proliferation of advanced public technology available for military use.
- The proliferation of weapons of mass destruction.
- Perceived increases in the proliferation and capability of unorthodox, or asymmetric, threats.
- Global and regional population trends.
- Global and regional trends in urbanization.[2]

As an experiment, if one were to deduce from all these concerns a picture of future urban conflict, it would be a dark vision indeed: unorthodox threats, challenging by asymmetric means the professional armed forces of the leading nations, in which the preferred locale of operations is the ever-expanding and volatile urban population and infrastructure of the developing nations.[3] Although most certainly overdrawn, this general appreciation of the operational future stands behind the several different perspectives on urban operations that have appeared lately in defense circles.

One of these perspectives, inevitably, argues that urban operations in the future will be so different as to constitute a wholly new form of military operations. This school of thought implies that experience is of little use and, indeed, that all we know of the history of conflict does not apply in this special case. As with all such arguments, this one has the virtue that no one can say with any certainty whether it is right or wrong.

At the opposite end of the argument, one hears that urban operations really are quite simple and are only a subclass of tactics. Urban operations demand hard, specialized training but little professional preparation. Some relatively simple technological advancements may prove useful, but there is "no silver bullet" where urban operations are

La Paz, Bolivia. Trends stop here?

concerned. As in the past, only expert soldiering will do. As evidence, one need only point to the many operations of this kind conducted by the United States and other nations in the half century since the Second World War. All that is needed now, so the argument goes, is to take account of lessons learned but forgotten along the way.[4]

Somewhere between these two perspectives lies a third, still in its infancy, but benefiting from enthusiasms created by the so-called "Military Technical Revolution." This view argues that technology has the power to render a difficult problem manageable. Perhaps not a single "silver bullet" but a combination of silver bullets will do. This argument holds a certain appeal by appearing to assuage official anxieties over friendly casualties; indeed, it hints at the possibility that death and destruction can be quarantined by precise means. There is reason to believe that this school of thought is winning more and more converts.[5]

Finally, no effort is required to find the traditional school of thought on urban operations. Indeed, most professional soldiers from the last several centuries would recognize the majority view in the leading armies today: it states that cities are no fit place for armies. Wars are never won in cities, and quite a few have been lost in them. Armies surrender every advantage they possess when they enter a city, and from the moment armies cross the line between landscape and cityscape, the environment turns against them. In war, cities are usually an annoyance and certainly a distraction from the main effort. Avoid them at all costs, or quarantine them from the rest of the war if they are unavoidable.[6]

So conventional wisdom makes a strong case for urban operations as a different and inferior kind of military action—so different as to constitute a different type of operation altogether. Of course, it is this particular environment, first of all, that works such a dominating influence over operations. An urban environment may turn otherwise routine operations into operations that are anything but routine. The most important feature of urban operations is that they *are* urban. That is why the first step to understanding them is to understand the unique environment in which they occur.

The Natural Environment and the Nature of the Urban Environment

The natural environment is an army's natural habitat. It is where an army is conceived, designed, equipped, and trained for optimum performance, where, given a choice, its commanders and soldiers will choose to function. Modern professional armies now divide the natural environment into five general kinds: the arctic, mountains, jungles, deserts, and woodlands.[7] There is general agreement among military professionals that each of these environments requires specific fighting doctrines, organizational adjustments, specially adapted arms and equipment, and specific training. Each of these environments makes particular demands upon soldiers and their commanders, but they are demands that can be analyzed and understood, anticipated, answered by planning, and capitalized upon in execution. Modern armies have learned that ignoring or minimizing the environmental context of their operations can be dangerous. Each of these natural environments has the power to defeat an unprepared army as surely as any enemy.

As physically different as these environments are from one another, they are alike in one respect *from a military point of view*. Before the armies arrive and operations commence, the pace of change in these environments appears to be relatively *static* (relatively, always, as combat engineers trying to bridge a recently flooded river might well attest). The interaction between a natural environment and a military force is usually limited and temporary, although military history records the most prodigious feats of military engineering when a general decided that nature was working against him. When General Grant attempted to circumvent the Mississippi River during the Vicksburg campaign, he followed in the footsteps of the Persian King Cyrus, who diverted the Euphrates River so that his warriors might wade into Babylon rather than assault its walls.[8] But even these military operations did not change the fundamental character of the landscape. Obviously, the natural environment can be changed, and vastly. But an army's purpose lies in another direction.

Once an army's mission brings it into contact with an urban environment, that army is best served by understanding these surroundings as well as any other place where it might act. At first glance, this rule seems theoretically desirable but practically impossible. Urban areas, so vastly different from one another and so individually complex, seem beyond the reach of a general, practical view that can be of use to a commander and his soldiers. One could say the same about mountains, but cities, like mountains, share certain common features—features that could play a critical role in any military operation. What are those common features?

The urban environment is, first of all, a human environment. That makes it different from all other forms of environment. An urban environment is not defined by its structures or systems but by the people who compose it. Philosophers once speculated that the earliest settlements arose "naturally," as if humans were guided into a place by some invisible structural law—a speculation for which no evidence exists. The earliest settlements known to history were not "natural" at all; they were established by human purpose and will.[9] Jericho, of biblical fame, is reckoned to be ten thousand years old, but its ruins show it to have been meant for defense as well as trade and worship. The nature, shape, and functions of any urban environment, regardless of time or place, are determined, in the final analysis, by those who create it and sustain it. What all this means is that the urban environment *reacts and interacts* with an army in a way that no natural environment could.

Because the urban environment is defined by a variety of human beings doing different work, it is a highly dynamic environment. Any human collective of any size, megalopolis or village, lives in a constant state of human and material motion. Anyone who stands at an intersection on a modern city street is struck first by its dynamism—the scale and pace of activity—but a closer look will show that this action is orderly. Not only is the intersection designed for its purpose, but people use it in a particular way. In return for their cooperation, the traffic moves, and they have a good chance of crossing the intersection in one piece. This social and material order—urban cohesion on a grand as well as a microscopic scale— enables a city to work as a city.[10]

Urban cohesion has often figured importantly in war and conflict. Soldiers throughout history have struggled against cities' power to resist, to withstand sieges lasting months or years, or to absorb the punishment of entire armies fighting within their precincts. Of course, the human quality that makes cities so resilient under stress can also be a source of vulnerability. Being chiefly human, cities can be killed. The final destruction of Carthage in 146 B.C. has come to stand for all cities killed by war. The Roman senators demanded the obliteration of Carthage when their legions finally took it after years of fighting. Ninety percent of the population had been killed or starved to death. The survivors were sold into slavery. The buildings were pulled down. The barren ground was sown with salt, but this was merely a gratuitous insult. Without Carthagenians, the Roman senators knew, there would be no Carthage.[11]

Cities are, after all, built to function in peace.[12] Once established, cities operate at a certain pace and rhythm unique to themselves, depending on the vitality of their social and material cohesion.

Furthermore, the process by which a city lives is not a degenerative but a regenerative one. Left to their own devices, cities do not decline. They persist.[13] But it is also true that, at some point, equally unique to a given city, a city's adaptive power can be overwhelmed, its cohesion disrupted. Natural disasters, industrial disasters, civil disorder, military conflict, or outright war—any or all of these can test a city's common systems and functions. At some point, the city begins to disorganize itself. The machinery of the essential and the commonplace—civil order, power, distribution of food and water, transport, medical care, communications—grinds toward an eventual halt. Then, the city *in extremis* becomes a different entity altogether—a place now hostile to its original reason for existence.

To appreciate how cities behave in war, we first have to see how they behave at rest, so to speak.

The Natural History of Cities

Cities form such a common backdrop of modern life everywhere that we rarely if ever see them in an analytical light. That, we can leave to urban planners, architects, civil engineers, and other experts. They make it possible for the rest of us to be at ease in the city, to function in that environment without quite understanding it.

The commander whose force is about to become entangled with a city has no such option. He must be able to understand the city from a *military point of view*—quite a different view from that taken by a resident or even an urbanologist. Seen as a military problem, an elevated expressway curving through a central urban core district (as one does in Houston) is a problem different in kind from the one considered by the planner who designed it. Seen as a military problem in 1945, Berlin's beautiful central park, the *Tiergarten,* posed an obstacle that required the attention of an entire Soviet army. In short, the commander must be prepared to "read" the city before him just as he would read a pastoral scene that could become a Somme. Knowing about cities in general, how their structures relate to their functions, and appreciating how those functions change under different circumstances are good first steps toward developing this professional skill.

In the urbanized world of the present, it is difficult to imagine a time when cities did not dominate human life as they do now. Once, cities were rare, and they were small. Ancient cities seldom had more than a few thousand inhabitants. Very important cities—Baghdad, Aleppo, Nineva, Ur—covered fewer than a thousand acres. A very few, truly

Photograph not available.

A suburban Siegfried Line, somewhere in Florida

exceptional cities—the world cities of their time—began to appear in the third millennium B.C.[14] When the Greek historian Herodotus gave us his description of fifth century Babylon, the city was already 2,400 years old, much besieged and much captured. East of Babylon, in the great river valleys of the Indus and the Hwang-Ho, cities as great as anywhere grew up: Mohenjo-Daro, Delhi, Nanjing, Canton, Beijing. The few great cities of the ancient Mediterranean were smaller—Constantinople, Alexandria, Athens—but still could count several hundred thousand people within their walls.[15] At the height of its classical growth in the fourth century B.C., Athens was said to have contained at least 200,000 people of all classes and kinds from their known world. Already the Greeks had coined the word *megalopolis*, but the city given this name had a population only one-fifth as large as Athens itself. To the Athenians, their own city was *metropolis*—the mother city.

Metropolis is a term that ought not be taken too literally, however: cities have assumed any number of shapes, so many that only the most general typologies are possible. In general, cities are built to meet the requirements of the place and day. Societies in which religious or secular power is highly concentrated seem to have a particular fondness for the radial design—all roads leading to and from the center of power, as if the power is magnified by the flow of social activity. Baghdad was designed by the Abbasid Caliph al-Mansur in 762 A.D. to be a round city, with his palace as the epicenter, enclosed by walls. These were protected by his army's barracks, also protected by a wall, which was itself surrounded by residential quarters protected by a third circuit of walls. The whole city was to have a radius of two miles. Beyond the outer walls were the bazaars. If the city actually conformed to al-Mansur's plans, it did not do so for long. Within a century, its population had reached a million. By one estimate, it was the largest city in the world during that period.[16] By then, Baghdad had come to resemble any number of other *medinas*, whose designs have often been characterized as "irregular."

As a city form, the *medina* can be found from the Indus to the Atlantic. Rules and customs guiding the shape of Islamic *medinas* were taken from the Qur'an and related traditions. They perpetuated the vision of the *medina* as a private place in which the family had sovereignty and took precedence over public functions. The primary structure in such towns is the neighborhood—the *hara* in Cairo and Damascus, the *hawma* in Algiers. The residences making up the neighborhoods show a blank, unadorned face to the streets outside and instead open inward upon a court. To those unaccustomed to such a place, housing might seem to have developed without reference to public mobility, but it would be more correct to say that the reference is different. It was possible for a street to be captured over time by the gradual encroachment of neighborhoods. Houses might extend themselves like a bridge over a street; one or both ends of a street might be given iron gates to be closed at night, or one end might be blocked completely, to prevent through traffic. One authority estimates that in Ottoman-era Cairo and Aleppo nearly 50 percent of the streets were dead-ends. Even so, streets were to obey certain forms themselves. One form in particular, derived from an aphorism of the Prophet, required that a street be wide enough for two working camels to pass—seven cubits. This rule was often honored in the breach. Secondary and tertiary streets were dark, narrow, winding, and, in original form, unhealthy in the extreme and vulnerable to fire. But *medinas* are not merely jumbled residences and neighborhoods. The mosque and the market, or *souk*, always have central places in the town where major thoroughfares can be joined to them, radiating outward, toward the countryside. The old *medinas* look disorganized because their form is irregular. But that is not the same as saying that *medinas* are irrational and therefore cannot be understood by virtue of their designs. Far from it.[17]

If there is a universal form for cities, it must be the *grid*, lines of streets at right angles to one another, a design urban planners call "orthogonal." Evidence of towns designed along the pattern of a grid can be found in all periods and places: the grid belongs to no one and to everyone. Often stigmatized as unimaginative, it is the most adaptable of any organized urban form. Grids can form the core of cities that guard mountain defiles, anchor seaports, and occupy hillsides or hilltops, as well as any topography in between. A grid can take over, in effect, from a city whose original radial design was appropriate for a particular location that it has outgrown. A city designed as a grid can be artless and authoritarian, but so can any other design. Designs do not determine the character of a given city. They reflect it.[18]

Whatever the early city's design, a wall was likely to protect it. City walls seem to be as old as cities. The oldest known city, ten thousand-year-old Jericho, was enclosed by a huge stone wall. Babylon's famous wall, with its hundred gates, was said to run eleven miles in all. A little later, about 1200 B.C., the Thebans had their hundred-gate wall as well, while in China, at Soochow about 430 B.C., walls enclosed more than a thousand hectares. By 700 A.D., China had seen one of the greatest city walls ever built at Chang'an, enclosing a thirty-square-mile area, along with one million inhabitants.[19]

Walls served more than a simple defensive purpose. As Lewis Mumford has observed, the city wall "made almost compulsory" the unification of "functions that had heretofore been scattered and unorganized"—"shrine, spring, village, market, stronghold."[20] Walls also served notice to those who wished to enter that one had to fit his conduct to customs and laws within. Market towns found walls to be useful control points for the collection of tariffs regulating trade and traders. Larger municipalities would specifically define the range of their authority by the circuit of their wall. Paris' own "tax wall" persisted well into the modern age. As for the military advantages conferred by walls, walled cities seemed to attract conquerers as much as deter them. Isfahan's experience, with its twelve miles of walls, was not unusual: in 1387, Tamerlane took it and slaughtered all 70,000 of its residents.[21] The same fate befell walled cities the world over.

The Greek cities had created colonial miniatures of themselves since the ninth century B.C. *Metropolis* was less a term of endearment than a practical description. Each of the Athenian colonies had an *agora*, or public market, just as in the original. These *agorae* were divided into trading circles, or *cycloi*, in which certain goods were marketed. The fish market, for instance, was the *icthyopolis*. Watching over the whole was the shrine to the gods, the *acropolis*, which always found commanding ground and, when the situation warranted, could be employed as a citadel. The situation often warranted that.[22]

In some way, all cities performed (and still perform) one or more specific functions: habitats, monuments to religious or secular power, trade, defense, safety. How localities attended to these functions varied according to immediate circumstances, but the functions themselves attracted people away from the solitude of the countryside to the cities. It was the magnetic effect of cities that Aristotle wanted us to appreciate when he wrote that "men come together in the city to live; they remain there in order to live the good life."[23]

Rome followed Athens' example famously, ruthlessly, successfully for a time. The city began its life very deliberately when, in the third century B.C., King Servius laid out a rectangle of one thousand acres and arranged for it to be enclosed with a wall wide enough at the top for two chariots abreast. The whole was quartered by two avenues, laid on the north-south and east-west axes. Before Rome's imperial career was over, it would seed more than 5,000 towns throughout the Mediterranean to Asia Minor. The Roman "New Towns" were built according to the standard of the Metropolis, a pattern specified as 2,400 feet long by 1,600 feet wide, that would not contain more than 50,000 inhabitants. Later on, the bivouacs of the Legions used exactly this design, and some of the towns settled by the Romans really began as little more than temporary military camps. Although the Romans hoped their New Towns would be as disciplined as legionary bivouacs, never were rules violated more lustily.[24]

Indeed, the idea that the plan for a town, once laid down, would be followed faithfully, then and evermore, has been a persistent one throughout history, and one just as persistently violated. Most cities, regardless of the intent or plan or vision at origin, are best viewed as the product of successive plans, overlaid on one another, or stitched together across an obliging landscape (or an altered landscape, as the case may be). They grow by accretion, phases that are the urban equivalent of a geologist's sedimentary layers or a botanist's tree rings. This process can be seen in Cairo's history. Invading Muslim armies established a camp, Fustat, in 641 on the east bank of the Nile. A century later, Fustat fell to the Abbasids, who established a new camp, El Askar, slightly to the northeast. Another century later, a rebellious local governor ordered a new headquarters built north of El Askar, which he would call al-Qata. In 967, yet another invasion occurred, this time by radicals from the west who put up another walled town still farther north that would celebrate their success. This town they would call "The Victorious," or al-Qahira. This chain of closely related settlements was finally bound together when, after 1169, the area was reconquered and a citadel was built immediately to the east. Fustat, El Askar, al-Qata, and al-Qahira eventually merged to become Cairo.[25]

Rome occupies a special place in the history of cities: it was the first to reach a population of one million. This, it likely did in the year 100 A.D. To the east, other cities were certainly on their way to a million people: Chang'an, in China, probably reached a million by the eighth century A.D.; Baghdad may have had a million inhabitants when the Mongols sacked it in 1258.[26] When a city approached this magnitude, how to accommodate growth became a preoccupying question. Since the challenge was progressive, not merely episodic, there was no final solution, only a series of adjustments, each of which sustained equilibrium for one moment more, until the next challenge. Six centuries after the Servian Walls laid down the outline of Rome's ambitions, the city had far outgrown its original limits. The new Aurelian wall went up in 274 A.D. to protect an area more than three times that of the original, but even then the total area of Rome, beyond and within the new walls, was nearly five thousand acres.[27] Of course, the character of these adjustments was determined by local needs. An outsider might be shocked by the solution of the moment, but the solution would not be his to judge. Universal standards tend to be misleading in such questions.

With the imperial *metropolis* fast becoming the *megalopolis* after 100 A.D., Rome is for many the embodiment of imperial decadence, seeing in the ultimate "fall" of Rome larger "lessons" for civilization. What is much clearer, however, is that urban problems that seem of more recent vintage can be found very early in Rome, beginning with the problem of overcrowding and the Roman solution for it. Although the common Roman dwelling in the countryside was a one-family house, congestion in the central districts became a real problem as early as the third century B.C. Four hundred years later, less than 20 percent of the whole population lived in their own houses; one estimate shows that of the million inhabitants, 821,000 lived in tenements as many as six precarious stories high, the notorious *insula*. One century after that, there were 46,602 *insulae* on record, but only 1,700 or so single-family houses.[28] Significantly, these *insulae,* death-defying as they were, would set the limit for *vertical* city building until the invention of the elevator 1,500 years later.

Any given settlement, accommodating demands of growth, will pass a point at which self-sustainment is no longer possible. This point might best signify a town's transition to city, for while towns or villages may provide for themselves, cities must depend upon surrounding, lesser towns.[29] Cities never exist in a vacuum but only as part of a wider network of settlement. Cities have always grown outward, and even the earliest cities give evidence that, whatever their original boundaries, there were always settlements to be found at the fringe or just beyond.[30] In this respect, at least, Rome was quite typical. When the Romans used the word *suburbium*, it described a trading area surrounding the city equal to about one day's travel in any direction.[31] And, of course, the traffic between city and countryside was just as important to one as to the other, but at a certain stage, a local exchange was insufficient. A city requiring more than 200,000 tons of grain a year to feed itself, as Rome did, is too large to be sustained by any area less than imperial in scope. Just as clearly, the exchange was hardly equal. At some point, the *megalopolis* became *parasitopolis*, drawing more from its sustaining environment than it returned.

How, why, and when this early experience of urban gigantism began to decline has been a matter of argument since the event. What is not

A modern Medina

subject to dispute, however, is that beginning in the middle of the fourth century A.D., that decline did begin to tell upon Rome. By the ninth century, the city of a million had declined to a population of only 17,000 residents. Thereafter, its rate of growth lagged far behind that of other, newer cities. By the eighteenth century, Rome still had only about 50,000 inhabitants. For 1,600 years, no city in the west would equal Rome at its ancient best.[32]

Questions of Scale

When Rome was largest, global population growth was, of course, neither steady nor uniformly distributed. Some 64 percent of the world's people could then be found in Asia. Standing then at about 300 million people, surges in growth in one locale were offset by disease, famine, and other hardships elsewhere.[33] Over the course of sixteen centuries, disasters of truly monumental proportions recorded by history did not appreciably affect population growth. In one four-year period during the fourteenth century, the famous Black Death epidemic killed nearly one-fourth of Europe's entire population, and lesser but still horrendous epidemics were common well into the eighteenth century. Wars were never so effective at taking lives as disease, but the Thirty Years' War in the first half of the seventeenth century was shockingly bloodthirsty even by the standards of the age. Estimates are that upwards of 20 percent of Germany's population was consumed by the war. However, none of these demographic disasters was sufficiently powerful to reverse population growth. Between 1100 and 1500, the number of towns in Europe alone doubled, usually in association with the rise of centralized, royal power.[34] In any case, one generation's growth was more than sufficient to fill in the losses from war and plague. By 1750, the world's population had doubled after 1,600 years: it stood at 600 million.[35] But this was a truly historic moment when a population surge of unprecedented magnitude was about to begin.[36] Little more than half a century later, in 1804, the world's population reached its first billion.

London inaugurated the era of the megalopolis, becoming in 1801 the first western city since Rome to reach a population of one million. Then, only fifty years later, London added a second million. One century after London first broke Rome's old record, eleven such cities had grown up: Paris, Berlin, Chicago, New York, Philadelphia, Moscow, St. Petersburg, Vienna, Tokyo, and Calcutta.[37] Today, depending on whether one counts immediate or surrounding administrative divisions, there are probably more than two hundred cities in the world whose population easily exceeds one million citizens.[38]

Sir Peter Hall, the leading urbanologist and planner, believes it was not until after 1800 that cities "became big enough and complex enough to present real problems of urban organization."[39] When a city outruns its capacity to provide for itself, it has also attained a new stage of complexity. This is the point at which questions such as the competition between population and space take on a different complexion altogether. The point of complexity is a qualitative, not a quantitative point, not simply the difference between one fire station and several fire stations—to take a mundane example. Several fire stations raise the question of equitable placement or appropriate placement—which? The frequency of fires in a given urban area could just as easily be considered a social as well as a practical observation. One fire station requires only a volunteer company. With several fire stations, one begins to think about a permanent organization, with all the calculations and other details of management that would entail. Suddenly, a simple matter is elevated to a public matter. Reaching a point of complexity means not merely that there are more moving parts but that the moving parts move differently.[40]

A city's outer limits, for instance, had long been defined by how far a worker could commute on foot for one hour from the city's central districts, where most day work was to be found.[41] But when a city's growth made this impracticable, the alternatives were less and less conducive to civic—and also to public—health. The density of a city's core population would rise to alarming levels—alarming, especially, to those who saw in crowded cities every dangerous habit and sentiment ever cultivated by man since the Fall. Cities had always made an attractive stage for moralizing, but the cities of the Victorian age gave self-appointed promoters of right conduct more ammunition than they could have ever wanted.[42] One contemporary critic of urban life helpfully satired genteel attitudes toward cities and those who mostly populated them, attitudes that seem to have changed little since he isolated them in 1899. The given wisdom of the time consisted of six indictments: those born in the city dominate the poorest parts of the city; city-born make up most of the lower social classes; city-born make up a disproportionately large percentage of "degenerates, criminals, lunatics, and suicides"; cities in general have a low "rate of natural increase" and a high rate of "deficient" births; and therefore, the "city-class" is "incapable of self perpetuation"; notwithstanding all this, there are just as many country born as city born in a given city,

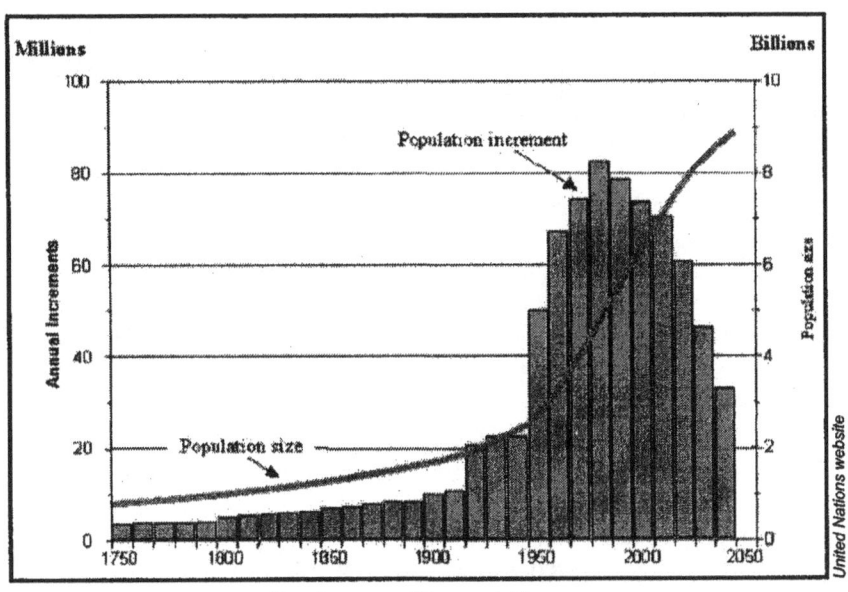

The demographic revolution

meaning, of course, that the better half is oppressed by the worst half of a city's population.[43]

No nineteenth-century cities were better demonstrations of the complexities of scale than London and Paris. Neither city could effectively absorb its rapid growth. Workers still had to live close to their work. The destitute and the poorest workers lived on top of one another in tenements that would have fitted perfectly in ancient Rome. London's 1851 census showed 2.8 million people living within 116 square miles. Within the concentrated slum areas of central London, whole families existed in rooms of eighty square feet. As might be expected in an area that produced 20,000 tons of horse manure each year, London had no effective municipal or sewer system, and so disease was rampant. Between 1831 and 1841, death rates in London actually rose by 50 percent. Life expectancy in ancient Rome had been reckoned at thirty-five years of age; in London in 1841, life expectancy overall was thirty-seven years of age, and lower still in slum areas.[44] Complexity and progress do not always go hand in hand.

Londoners visiting Paris in the midnineteenth century gasped, however, at what they considered uninhabitable congestion. During Baron Haussman's famous reconstruction of Paris at midcentury, the city was increasing its population from 1.3 million in 1850 to almost 2 million by 1870, reaching densities of 1,000 people per hundred acres in the central *arondissements*. Of course, the newest arrivals, always the poorest, were blamed. They were miserable by an act of will. Disease, crime, poverty, gang warfare, spasms of insurrectionary and near-insurrectionary violence: all this was in the nature of what one veteran Parisian called "the new barbarians."[45] None of this would have been unfamiliar to a nineteenth-century New Yorker, except that toward the end of the century, the poor in that city were the new immigrants who crowded onto the Lower East Side at a density of 260,000 per square mile (for a few blocks here, density ran as high as 1,700 per acre).[46]

Very likely, people have struggled to get out of cities as long as they have struggled to get in them. So the interaction between the city and its periphery would seem to be a straightforward one in which pressures on the city proper are relieved by its suburbs. But the demographic explosion after 1800 posed unprecedented burdens on the cities, and the way cities responded was by no means uniform.

Little could be done—was done—by any of these overburdened cities until a wholly new factor was introduced into the city environment. Long-standing ratios of urban time and space were to be turned on their head by the advent of public transportation systems. But the effects had to be within everyone's grasp, not merely that of the privileged classes, who in any case had never been constrained by the old systems. London began its first steps toward mass transportation in the 1840s and had a working system by 1863—the world's first.[47] But despite the innovation of "workmen's trains," which ran cheapest, earliest, and latest each day, a full generation would pass before day workers could afford to live very far from their work. The suburbs in England and America (and those who built them) profited by their access to these systems to become bastions of middle-class gentility, and they have so remained. Elsewhere, cities related to their suburbs quite differently. The continental elites, as a rule, refused to be tempted out of their cities. Once Paris was "renewed" by Baron Haussmann's reforms, rents in central Paris ran so high that workers were forced to abandon their slums for dense shantytowns at the edge of the city's limits. In Vienna, the creation of an industrial belt beyond the new *Ringstrasse* served the same purpose, if more humanely, of leaving the central city to the fashionable classes. Before long, more than thirty working class districts attached themselves to the industrial belt.[48]

The old ratios of urban time and space were to be redrawn on another plane as well: the vertical. The builder's art had not really advanced upward since antiquity. Real physical limits kept buildings below seven or eight stories at most; five stories was everywhere typical, from ancient Rome to modern Paris, London, and New York.[49] City skylines were flat, punctuated if at all by spires, minarets, victory monuments, or some ornamental structure not encumbered by habitual, practical use. Just as a city's outer limits had been set by how far a worker was likely to commute by foot, a similar limit seems to have influenced building heights: why build tall buildings anyway if people would not climb that far? Compounded with this social preference, the real risk of collapse or fire made tall buildings both unprofitable and undesirable. Thus, two changes were required, with progress in the one depending materially upon progress in the other. From the middle of the nineteenth century onward, and in America at first, the art of taller buildings and the art of the elevator advanced symbiotically. By 1900, the century of the skyscraper had arrived.[50]

For quite some time, all cities had been forced to apply themselves chiefly to sustaining urban mobility.[51] Reforms in public transportation during the nineteenth century had enabled the urban machine to run at a higher speed, volume, and distance. Momentous as these developments were, what followed worked new differences in how urbanites interacted with their world. The immediate agent of this change was the automobile, and the city that embraced this change most enthusiastically—and successfully—was Los Angeles. Municipal boosters in L. A. liked to depict their city as poised on the threshold of the future. By creating "the first mass motorized city on the planet," L. A. lived up to its billing.[52]

Los Angeles enjoyed several advantages that escaped older, eastern cities, not least of which was that it was small and relatively underdeveloped when the automobile made its debut. Like other rising American cities, L. A. had invested in public transportation; interurban rail lines connected several smaller communities with L. A.'s central business district. By the 1920s, all suburban roads led to L. A. in a radial network reaching as far out as thirty miles. And since developers would not risk building houses more than four blocks from a streetcar line, these lines were punctuated by bubbles of development and an occasional smaller community. In other words, Los Angeles was already a polycentric urban area ready made for the automobile age.[53]

Aristotle's ancient dictum on cities was about to be revised: people collected in cities, not so much to be together as to make the better life

Collection of The New-York Historical Society

Chicago, 1892. The city goes vertical.

20

that being together had made possible. Once cars enabled one to make a good life without contributing to urban congestion, Los Angelenos had a new choice to make: how far to live from one's place of work. Freedom of movement expanded greatly when one was not bound by the limited patterns and schedules of public transport systems. In effect, the automobile made it possible to construct one's own city, without reference to the city's organization.[54] If one desired, one could make a different city *every day*. Traditional points of reference, old calculations of time and space, no longer counted. Even before World War II, downtown L. A. began to decline; growth followed the suburbs. The rest of the United States seems to have followed L. A., as no doubt its early boosters would have wished: by 1990, more of the population of the United States was found in suburbs than in urban and rural areas combined.[55]

In light of this, it is interesting that suburbs and the way of life they produce attract little serious attention except by land developers and urban specialists. For most Americans, suburbs are so amorphous as to suggest no identifying features at all: political travel writer Robert Kaplan sees only a future marked by "vast suburban blotches separated by empty space."[56] However, it may be useful to think of them more concretely. First, suburbs are not cities themselves, but without cities there would be no suburbs. Today, the world over, cities have seen themselves surrounded by suburbs, whose combined population far outnumbers that of the city proper. The city of Rio de Janiero reported a population of 5.4 million in its most recent census, but the entire metropolitan region counted nearly as much again, 10.3 million people in all, distributed in fourteen different municipalities. Nevertheless, each suburb draws its economic and material and perhaps even spiritual sustenance from the metropolis—not from each other. Second, suburbs are smaller entities than their metropolis; not one of Rio's suburbs begins to approach Rio itself.[57] Third, because suburbs are smaller, they are also simpler, less complex. The complexity factor works in reverse here: there are fewer moving parts and the whole machine performs fewer operations. Finally, suburbs tend toward homogeneity, a certain kind of sameness with cohesive social properties that could be based on ethnicity or religion or economics or even ideology. Suburbs, simply, make it possible for urban populations to redivide and rearrange themselves. In this respect, Potomac, Maryland; Burbank, California; Westport, Connecticut; and Schaumberg, Illinois, are no different from Tokyo's Tama New City, Mexico City's Pedregal, Rio de Janiero's Neves, or Singapore's Johor. Each of these suburbs exists only in reference to the larger city. That reference is the suburb's *raison d'etre*.

Ten Cities and a Future

In October 1999, the world's population passed six billion. Only a dozen years had been required to add this latest billion, and only thirteen years before that, in 1974, the fourth billion was added. Compared to the great demographic surge beginning in 1750, the acceleration experienced by the world after 1950 was more powerful by several orders of magnitude. If, geologically speaking, 1750 registered 7.0 on the Richter Scale, 1950 was off the scale. By 1965, the growth rate of the global population was 2 percent per year. Five years later, the growth rate began to decline, so that today its stands at 1.31 percent per year, meaning that 1999 will record a global net gain in population amounting to 78 million people. Seen another way, the world's population has roughly doubled in less than forty years, a truly singular record in the history of population growth.

These figures, taken from a recent report by the United Nations, are derived from the best available data and can be regarded as authoritative descriptions of recent population trends. These data are also taken as the basis for calculations of future trends—quite a different proposition altogether. Of this year's new additions, for instance, it is estimated that 95 percent will live in less-developed regions, an estimate that seems as tenable as one could expect. In the same way, the UN's report estimates future growth rates and population distribution patterns as much as fifty years hence. By these estimates, the global population will approach 9 billion by the year 2054. Sixty percent of these people will reside in Asia, and Africa's present share of the total will have doubled to 20 percent by then. Europe, on the other hand, will contribute only 7 percent of the grand total, down to only one-third of its share during the heady days at the beginning of the twentieth century. Further, 46 percent of the world population is now urbanized, and by 2006, half of the world's people will live in cities. It is easy to jump to the conclusion, of course, that whatever the global future looks like will be determined mostly in Asia and Africa, and mostly in cities besides.[58]

These quantitative recitations can be impressive, seeming to convey unarguable facts. The possibility that all extrapolations should be regarded as educated guesses, hedged by technical nuance and sensible reservation by those who make them, is too often overlooked. In fact,

Megalopolis: an infrared satellite shot of New York City

the most populous regions of the world have *not* inevitably been the most powerful regions of the world. At the turn of the nineteenth century, while Asia was still being divided up by colonial powers, Asia's share of the global population was roughly the same as projections for the year 2054.[59] It also does not follow from these projections that cities are inherently unstable, that they are hotbeds of unrest, or that in some way they contain clues to the future of humanity in general.

The largest cities of the world defy generalized predictions of disaster. Some of these cities would be considered successful by any standard of measurement. Some would be considered spectacularly unsuccessful but for their unaccountable attraction to more and more inhabitants each year. Somehow, people find reasons to live in these cities too. As a group, however, these cities lend credence to the urbanographer's rule that, however good or bad, cities tend to persist.

The ten largest cities of the world, by the UN's latest count, contain between them more than 162 million people and rank this way, their population given in millions:

Tokyo	28.8
Mexico City	17.8
Sao Paulo	17.5
Bombay (Mumbai)	17.4
New York	16.5
Shanghai	14.0
Los Angeles	13.0
Lagos	12.8
Calcutta	12.7
Buenos Aires	12.3[60]

If there is a discernible urban future, one might expect to see it here first, where success and failure are so highly magnified by scale and complexity. What is more certain is that these cities embody the urban present more comprehensively than any other collection, which is why these warrant a closer inspection.

One notices first that Europe is not represented at all. North America contributes two cities. East Asia and South Asia have two cities each, while Latin America takes the overall lead with three cities. Africa has only one entry, that of Lagos. Of course, it would be all too easy to overstate the significance of this scheme, but it does bear out other UN projections that show less-developed nations producing larger urban agglomerations. In 1960, the three largest cities in the world were New York, Tokyo, and London, in that order. Twenty-five years later, the rankings were Tokyo, then Mexico City, and finally Sao Paulo. By 2015, according to this estimate, the three largest cities will be Tokyo (with 28.9 million), Bombay (with 26.2 million), and Lagos (with 24.6 million).[61]

All but two of these cities are of colonial origin, and one of those, Shanghai, despite being over a thousand years old, became a multinational possession in the nineteenth century when several Western powers established themselves in the heart of the city. What one sees as the old core of Shanghai today, with its decidedly European architecture, dates from this period of colonial subjugation. Of all these cities, only Tokyo had no colonial past, and even this is open to debate if one takes into account its occupation by the Allied powers following the Second World War.

All except one—Los Angeles—could be characterized as a premodern city; that is, the city dates its original configuration from before the advent of the industrial age. This is not mere historicism: cities whose core design was established before the introduction of the automobile, or even public transport systems, have been faced with herculean problems in adaptation. Los Angeles can be said to have escaped the worst of this challenge simply because, as late as the 1870s, it was still only a country village, with not quite six thousand inhabitants.

All but one of these giant cities is a port city or is one that has grown up in intimate relationship with a port, as in the cases of Tokyo and Yokohama, Sao Paulo and Santos. Only Mexico City is an inland city, beyond the sustenance of a seaport. Tokyo, New York City, Bombay, Calcutta, Shanghai and Lagos all have incorporated islands into their metropolitan areas. Tokyo continues, in effect, to create islands in its bay to accommodate growth in a highly constricted geographic zone. Bombay was originally settled upon a chain of seven islands. Lagos began its career on four islands in the Bight of Benin. Calcutta grew up in the Ganges estuary and has been unable to solve season flooding problems. Shanghai claims upwards of thirty islands within its metropolitan area.

Indeed, no city yet has grown so large that it can afford to dismiss the physical challenges of its locale. Three of these cities live under a real threat of earthquake—Tokyo, Los Angeles, and Mexico City. Tokyo suffered an earthquake in 1923; not even the Allied bombing campaign of early 1945 destroyed as much of the city and killed as many of its inhabitants. Mexico City's most recent earthquake, in 1985, killed several thousand people and injured thousands more. Los Angeles' Northridge earthquake of 1994 cost few lives but more money.

Even today, one can see how the original designs of these cities work upon the whole. Central Tokyo's radial organization dates from its premodern origins as a fortress town, and its later evolution as Japan's imperial city ensured the persistence of a central precinct where all roads converge. Major traffic arteries today obey the same scheme, and were Tokyo not supplemented by one of the most sophisticated public transportation systems in the world, the city would not move.

Mexico City, like Tokyo, owes its overall configuration to the surrounding topography. In Mexico City's case, the valley of Mexico itself formed the original container, just as it had for the Aztecan capital on whose ruins it was built. Like any number of other colonial towns of Spanish or Portuguese origin, Mexico City's core is formed by a plaza that centralizes the functions of government, religion, and trade and around which one finds various neighborhoods organized by ethnicity, class, or occupation.

In some instances, such as that of Bombay, topography limits expansion. The original site of the city occupies an area of only twenty-six square miles and is effectively separated from the mainland by its harbor. In the modern city, the lack of space has encouraged the development of a vertical city after the fashion of Hong Kong and Singapore, cities that suffer the same problem. In these cases, the population density naturally increases, but what may be called the "functional density"—the concentration of sustaining goods and services—increases as well and produces even higher degrees of human, material, and organizational complexity. Towns and smaller cities naturally operate at a smaller pitch, a lower tempo, than larger places. The higher tempo of cities is possible because, over time, their populations have provided for it by creating these sustaining—and frequently interlocking—systems. A city's capacity to manage these systems is not won overnight. In effect, the systems grow as the city grows. Tokyo's subway system, for instance, could never have been built as a single piece; the system—and those who use it—had to grow together, so to speak. Tokyo's success might well be easier to understand than Calcutta's, with a population density of nearly 62,000 per square mile. But even as "one of the most ill-serviced and chaotic metropolises of the world," Calcutta continues to operate. By any standard, that cannot fail to impress.[62]

Modern global urbanism on this gigantic scale naturally poses the question of whether there is a finite limit of growth, whether there is some undiscovered critical point, beyond which a city's fundamental cohesion is endangered? But cities have been unsuccessful before and have been disappearing from the map since antiquity, not because of size or complexity or what might be supposed as inherent structural weaknesses, but because their context changed: a shrine moved, a water source dried up, a prince chose a different capital. Much more commonly, as one urbanographer has written, "cities in their physical aspect are stubbornly long-lived." It is much more likely that if there are limits to urbanism, they will be human, not artificial ones.[63] In that respect, the fundamental substance of cities is precisely that of war itself.

In the future, professional soldiers the world over will be more likely to find themselves operating—and sometimes fighting—in cities than in any other environment. The three wars fought by the United States since 1945 are the last gasps of a dying military tradition in which immense armies maneuver against one another over vast, unencumbering landscapes. A military future of the kind discussed here certainly does not correspond to the age-old self-image soldiers prefer to cultivate. Heroic charges are a bad idea when one is in contact with an enemy a few meters away in a darkened basement filled with concrete wreckage and noncombatants. But if armies do not shed themselves of their quickly obsolescing ways, there will be no shortage of "last stands."

No single moment in history was ever all new or all old. Looking backward, we can see that modern war began turning slowly toward urban operations again during the Second World War and that this trend has gained momentum ever since. Armies the world over have a wealth of their own experience to complement the great weight of historical knowledge. But experience is not the same as knowledge: the question to be answered now is what the armies have learned from their own experience and, better yet, as Bismarck would have said, the experience of others. The next part of this study addresses that question.

Notes

1. Military Operations in the Continental United States are not included in this working definition. Constitutional, political, and social questions require that these operations be considered separately from all other military operations.

2. See, for instance, US Army Science Board, *Final Report of the Army Science Board Ad Hoc Group of Military Operations in Built-Up Areas (MOBA)* (Washington, D. C.: Office of the Assistant Secretary of the Army [RDA], January 1979), which cites several of these concerns.

3. See Ralph Peters, "The Culture of Future Conflict," *Parameters* (Winter 1995): 18-27; Eliot A. Cohen, "A Revolution in Warfare," *Foreign Affairs* 75, no. 2 (March-April 1996): 37-54; and Edward N. Luttwak, "Toward Post-Heroic Warfare," *Foreign Affairs* 74, no. 3 (May-June 1995): 109-22. Lastly, see Ralph Peters, "The Future of Armored Warfare," and Paul Van Riper and Robert H. Scales, "Preparing for War in the 21st Century," *Parameters* 27, no. 3 (Autumn 1997): 50-59, 4-26. Indeed, most of the Autumn 1997 issue of *Parameters* may be said to be an exercise in this sort of pseudo-prognostication.

4. A view that may fairly be said to include that of the United States Marine Corps' doctrinal concept, "Urban Warrior." For a public view, comparing the Marines and the Army's work in this field, see Tom Ricks, "Urban Warfare: Where Innovation Hasn't Helped," *Wall Street Journal*, 12 October 1999, 10.

5. Including, most notably, John Keegan. See his "Please, Mr Blair, never take such a risk again," *London Daily Telegraph*, 6 June 1999 (see also http: www.telegraph.co.uk, Internet).

6. See, for instance, Major General Robert H. Scales, Jr., "The Indirect Approach: How U. S. Military Forces Can Avoid the Pitfalls of Future Urban Warfare," in *Future Warfare* (Carlisle Barracks, PA: U. S. Army War College, 1999), 173-85.

7. One might even add the "aerial environment" or the "maritime environment."

8. See Ulysses S. Grant, *Memoirs and Selected Letters* (New York: The Library of America, 1990), 292-304. As for the campaign of Cyrus, Paul Bentley Kern's *Ancient Siege Warfare* (London: Souvenir Press, 1999), 59, has an account taken chiefly from Herodotus.

9. Spiro Kostof, *The City Shaped: Urban Patterns and Meanings Through History* (London: Thames and Hudson, 1991; paperback 1999), 53. See also, Lewis Mumford, *The City in History* (New York: MFJ Books, 1961), 31.

10. See Mumford's comments on this dynamic equilibrium, which he views as a degenerative, not a regenerative process, in his *City in History*, 31.

11. The ancient and common custom of razing cities is discussed in Kern's *Ancient Siege Warfare*, 323-51.

12. While it is true that some cities had very warlike beginnings as military camps or fortresses, these places grew beyond their narrow original purpose or they did not survive for very long. Today, few cities would claim a singular purpose or would want to. Saudi Arabia's King Khalid Military City comes to mind, but it is more properly classed a military base. Elsewhere, military bases have taken on many of the characteristics of a small city, but these commonly depend for many of their functions on the communities that surround them.

13. Spiro Kostof, *The City Assembled: The Elements of Urban Form Throughout History* (Boston: Little Brown, 1999), 250.

14. See Gideon Sjoberg's classic, *The Preindustrial City: Past and Present* (New York: The Free Press, 1960), 33-64, for a survey of the archaeology of the earliest cities.

15. Kostof, *The City Shaped*, 37. See also Mumford, *City in History*, 235. As Kostof notes, no one now argues that the city had its origin in a single place, as scholars once believed.

16. Tertius Chandler and Gerald Fox, *3000 Years of Urban Growth*, with a foreword by Lewis Mumford (New York and London: Academic Press, 1974), 221, 363. See also, Kostof, *The City Shaped*, 12-13.

17. Sjoberg, *The Preindustrial City*, 91-97; and Kostof, *The City Shaped*, 62-64, 106. A good deal of commentary on whether cities are ever "unplanned" seems to turn upon who does the planning. By adopting a presentist standard—that is, that nothing is planned unless a city planning commission does it—urbanographer Howard J. Nelson is able to characterize Los Angeles' growth from 1900 to 1990 as "mostly unplanned." See his essay on "Los Angeles," in *Microsoft Encarta Encyclopedia 99*, CD-ROM.

18. Kostof, *The City Shaped*, 62-64.

19. Tercius Chander and Gerald Fox, *3000 Years of Urban Growth* (New York and London: Academic Press, 1974), 79-82, 291. See also, Sjoberg, *The Preindustrial City*, 91-98.

20. Mumford, *The City in History*, 31.

21. Chandler and Fox, *3000 Years*, 226.

22. Sir Peter Hall, *Cities in Civilization* (New York: Pantheon, 1998), 38.

23. Virtually every modern urbanographer finds a way to quote Aristotle's remark. See Mumford, *City in History*, 111.

24. Hall, *Cities in Civilization*, 624-25.

25. Kostof, *The City Assembled*, 25.

26. Sir Peter Hall, *Cities in Civilization*, 621. Inevitably, there is disagreement about the precise time Rome achieved the one million mark. The figures given here represent a compromise between extremes of date and number. All sources agree that Rome was bigger than any other city, so much bigger that it constituted a real anomaly in the ancient urban world. Kostof, *The City Shaped*, 37. See also, Mumford, *City in History*, 235.

27. Mumford, *City in History*, 235.

28. Hall, *Cities in Civilization*, 621-27.

29. Ibid., 611.

30. Fernand Braudel, *The Structures of Everyday Life,* volume 1, *Civilization and Capitalism, 15th to the 18th Century,* trans. by Sian Reynolds (New York: Harper and Row, 1981), 481. See also, Kostof, *The City Shaped*, 37, who argues flatly that "cities come in clusters."

31. Hall, *Cities in Civilization*, 649.

32. Chang' an, in China, may have reached the million mark by the eighth century. Baghdad may have had a million inhabitants when the Mongols sacked it in 1258. Beijing was probably the largest city in the world when London passed it in the nineteenth century. Kostof, *The City Shaped,* 37. See also, Mumford, *City in History,* 235.

33. At the same time, Europe contributed only 21 percent of the total, Africa 13 percent. After 150 years, Europe's contribution to the total had risen to 25 percent, while Asia's share had dropped to 57 percent, and Africa's only 8 percent. United Nations, "The World at Six Billion" (New York: United Nations Population Division, Department of Economic and Social Affairs, 12 October 1999), available also at Internet.

34. Kostof, *The City Shaped,* 108-10.

35. Ibid.

36. Until 1900, the rate of world population growth remained at about .0002 percent per annum, or roughly twenty million people a year. The Population Council, "Population," *Microsoft Encarta Encyclopedia 99*, p. 4, CD-ROM.

37. Mumford, *City in History*, 529.

38. David Crystal, ed., *The Cambridge Factfinder,* 3d edition (Cambridge: Cambridge University Press, 1998), 201.

39. Hall, *Cities in Civilization*, 618.

40. Sjoberg, *The Preindustrial City*, 106. "The wheels must turn at just the right moment," Sjoberg writes.

41. Kostof, *The City Assembled*, 59; Hall, *Cities in Civilization*, 612.

42. A fair example, now generally recognized as such, is Lewis Mumford's major work, *The City in History*, which, though path breaking in many respects, suffered in general from an apocalyptic view of cities as the chief mechanisms of a civilization's death. His concept of the "Necropolis," detailed on page 242, was particularly appealing to those who shared his prejudices.

43. These are the criticisms of Adna Ferrin Weber, first detailed in Weber's classic, *The Growth of Cities in the Nineteenth Century* (New York: Macmillan, 1899), reproduced in Don Martindale, "Prefatory Remarks: The Theory of the City," in Max Weber, *The City*, trans. by Don Martindale and Gertrud Neuwirth (Glencoe, Illinois: The Free Press, 1958), 17.

44. Hall, *Cities in Civilization*, 648, 658, 684, 695, 701.

45. David P. Jordan, *Transforming Paris: The Life and Labors of Baron Haussmann* (Chicago: University of Chicago Press, 1995), 93-96.

46. Hall, *Cities in Civilization*, 709, 753.

47. William C. Graeub, "Public Transportation," *Microsoft Encarta Encyclopedia 99*, CD-ROM.

48. Kostof, *The City Assembled*, 50-61. There is more than a hint of resentment by urbanographers and historians toward the advent of transportation as not only an important factor in city planning and sustainment but as a transcendent factor—a factor bearing such weight upon the whole subject that urban planning has been subordinated to traffic management and little else.

49. Masonry foundations could bear relatively little weight for instance, and framing materials before the use of iron and steel left much to be desired.

50. Hall, *Cities in Civilization*, 770-78.

51. Mumford, *City in History*, 391.

52. Hall, *Cities in Civilization*, 804.

53. Ibid., 806, 815.

54. A point made by Spiro Kostof in *The City Shaped*, 69, as well as by Robert Fishman in his *Bourgeois Utopias: The Rise and Fall of Suburbia* (New York: Basic Books, 1987), 185, among others.

55. Kenneth T. Jackson, "America's Rush to Suburbia," *The New York Times,* 9 June 1996, quoted in Robert Kaplan, *An Empire Wilderness: Travels into America's Future* (New York: Random House, 1999), 23.

56. Kaplan, *An Empire Wilderness,* 23. It is quite amazing to see suggested in a leading professional military journal, for instance, that cities could "secede" from their countries or that suburbs could "secede" from their cities; this sort of prognostication betrays a fundamental misunderstanding of urban history and development.

57. Robert B. Kent, "Rio de Janeiro," *Microsoft Encarta Encyclopedia 99,* CD-ROM.

58. United Nations, "The World at Six Billion" (New York: United Nations Population Division of the Department of Economic and Social Affairs, 1999), b-2, b-3; available at <http://www.un.org/popin> (retrieved 1999).

59. One need only remember the West's reaction to the Japanese economic miracle of the late 1980s and early 1990s: it seemed inevitable that the Japanese economy would prosper forever and mainly at the expense of Western economies. Western experts were dispatched, books were written, movies were even made. All purported to explain the mysteries of Japanese culture and

behavior in order to understand the keys to Japanese success. But Japan's recession immediately thereafter spoiled all the predictions. History intervened. See, for example, Jonathon Rauch, *The Outnation: A Search for the Soul of Japan* (Boston: Little Brown, 1992); James Fallows, *Looking at the Sun: The Rise of the Near East Asian Economic and Political System* (New York: Vintage Books, 1994); Michael Crichton, *Rising Sun* (New York: Ballantine Books, 1992), which spawned a successful motion picture; Ian Buruma, *Behind the Mask* (New York: Ballantine Books, 1984), very likely the best of contemporary western social analyses; and, for a convenient summary, Walter LaFeber, *The Clash: U. S-Japanese Relations Throughout History* (New York: W. W. Norton, 1997), 357-405.

60. UN, "The World at Six Billion," p. t31. htm. (See note 33).

61. UN, *World Urbanization Prospects: The 1996 Revision*, 1997 <www.prb.org/pubs, notebook/slide 18.jpg> (retrieved 1999).

62. Ashok K. Dutt, "Calcutta," *Microsoft Encarta Encyclopedia 99*, pp. 5, 8, CD-ROM.

63. Kostof, *The City Shaped*, 30.

A culmination point in Sarajevo

Part Two

Under Fire: Urban Operations in Perspective

The Nature and Conduct of the Siege

As long as there is war and as long as there are cities, there will be sieges. Now, the word conjures up castles, drawbridges, moats, catapults and battering rams, desperate assaults up the curtain walls. As a mode of operation, the siege seems hopelessly out of military fashion, frozen somewhere deep in the Middle Ages. But the siege has shown itself to be long-lived, highly adaptable to time and place. At certain times in the history of war, the siege was preeminent, the preferred mode of operation; at other times, the siege fell so far out of favor that it was relegated to the dustiest shelves of the military art, of antiquarian interest only.

To say that the concept of a siege is antithetical to the self-image of modern military establishments is an understatement. Today, at best, the siege represents a distraction. At worst, a siege is taken as evidence of a misfired plan, an incompetent commander, an offensive ground to a halt, initiative lost, a loss of control. Modern armies prefer to act as if they have outgrown the siege, but even as this line is being written, a siege is under way in the Transcaucasus, well into its third month. Its operational and tactical sequences would have been understood thousands of years ago, even before history began. And that is why we will begin there.

Ancient walls did not only protect their cities. Walls, even the flimsiest, aided the regulation of trade and customs, the control of traffic, the maintenance of public order, the protection (or the containment) of certain inhabitants—and other functions as well. But walls were also the means by which the city could defend itself when nothing else could, or would, defend it. Perhaps the city's defenders were real, full-time soldiers, a heavy garrison, well trained, fully provisioned, well led. Or perhaps not. Perhaps those who claimed the city as their own decided they would rather spend their surplus on walls rather than a permanent garrison that produced nothing but idlers when they were not fighting. If the walls were thick enough, high enough, well designed, protected by extra curtain walls or moats or some other device, perhaps those defending the city need only know how to fight just well enough to hold on. Perhaps the walls could take the place of good training, even good leaders. With these advantages, perhaps the city could hold out just long enough for the enemy to lose so many of their own soldiers that they would lose heart for the fight, too. Then the city could return to normal. Rarely did events run such a course.

Cities bring out the worst in armies, and armies bring out the worst in cities. To an army, a city in the way offered the prospect of unopposed violence and plunder. To a city, an army was a monster, beyond the reach of sentiment and therefore to be treated as such, to be kept out if possible or, if not, to be killed without mercy. Of course, to a city, it was always better that the attacking army be destroyed then and there, for fear it would return later, stronger, less-easily dissuaded from its purpose, less merciful should it succeed where once it had failed.

As the record of warfare makes plain, these were prevailing attitudes, not in the least exceptional; in the clash between city and army, these attitudes could be depended upon, even hoped for. Perhaps they will seem extreme, but if we look carefully at our own century's record of one hundred million war deaths, we should not be so shocked. Human behavior has always been equal to the savagery of war, no matter how extreme. And in the beginning, no other form of early combat posed the test of intense, prolonged, unremitting violence as did combat in and against cities.

The sight of an approaching army ranked almost on a par with such natural disasters as famine, pestilence, flood, or earthquake. If the oncoming army did not seem quite so disastrous, that was only because it was possible to negotiate with an army. Most often, however, armies did not behave much differently from an element of nature, for the fact always remained that the city had no bargaining power and that in these transactions the city was always on the defensive and the army always enjoyed the initiative. It was possible, theoretically, for a city to fight off an attacker, and there are records of heroic, steadfast resistance that simply wore down the besieger's will. The great king Nebuchadnezzar, legend has it, besieged the city of Tyre for thirteen years without success, but such cases are remarkably few.[1] Better always to assume that, sooner or later, one's city would fall and be rendered prostrate before the enemy, the most dangerous of all times in combat.

Under these circumstances, the courses of action open to a city were few and all unappealing. An immediate capitulation, offered well before the arrival of the enemy's main body, was the most ingratiating of courses. Throwing the city on the mercy of the attacking army was always a highly dubious proposition. Not wanting to cast honor completely to the winds, the next course was to resist for the sake of face, pride, or self-respect, to force the attacking army into the inconvenience of deploying and arraying for the fight and suffering through a few assaults before giving up. Of course, this tests the enemy's capacity for forgiveness a little more, and the city might be made to pay for its impertinence.

A city confident of its power and the vitality of its citizens might elect to fight, however. Here, at least, there was the possibility of survival, not so much winning as not losing. From the attacking army's point of view, this was the least desirable of options. Not only might it mean a long siege, but it might also mean increasing vulnerability to a relieving army. If the city would not move, neither could the army. And once the army began to take root along the siege lines, its own vitality began to decline as well.

The final option for the city was tantamount to suicide—fighting to the bitter end. This was a course of action not quite so irrational as it might seem. The consequences of defeat were hardly more appealing; indeed, there was not much one could lose.

The victorious army essentially had three options, however. First, the army could kill everyone in the city. The ancient Assyrian king Ashurnasirpal II (883-859 B.C.) took twenty-one cities in six different campaigns during his reign. In nine of these, his imperial scribes recorded, all the inhabitants were killed. In six others, they wrote, "many were slain."[2] This was an option often followed. Attempts at completely destroying a city are found throughout history on virtually every continent. In 614 B.C., everyone in Jerusalem, all 92,000 people, were either killed or carried off. The Roman legions may have killed as many as 70,000 in London in 200 B.C. In the Christian Era, the number of attempted city killings goes up, especially during the Mongol depredations of Asia Minor and Persia during the thirteenth and fourteenth centuries: first in Turkestan came Bakasaghum—40,000 killed, then Samarkand, 30,000, and Merv, which is noted as "completely destroyed," as was Kirovobad, in Armenia. In 1258, Baghdad itself, with perhaps 100,000 residents, was destroyed, and thirty-nine years later, all of Damascus's 100,000 inhabitants were either killed or enslaved. Those who survived the massacres were sent to Samarkand as slaves, but only half of those managed the thousand-mile walk. The town itself was abandoned. Toward the end of the fourteenth century, another spasm of warfare broke out in the region: Tamerlane's massacre of Isfahan in 1390 has already been noted; three years later, his army took the city of Balkh. "All" were

Ruins of the ancient fortress of Gur (in what is now Iran)

killed, the record notes grimly. Farther to the east, India was not spared the ravages of invasion either but, in addition, frequently suffered from sectarian wars unequaled for their viciousness. In the city of Chittor, 30,000 males were killed in one day of fighting between Hindu and Moslem in 1303. Twenty years later, at Warangal, 50,000 defenders of the city killed their own women and children for fear they would be taken by the attacking Moslem army. Then, they fought to the death.[3]

As the men of Warangal seemed to fear, even if the victors put the city's men to the sword, there was no assurance that their wives and children would be spared. That was the second possible course of action: a city's defenders, having acquitted themselves honorably, could hope at least that their survivors would not be abused. But that was the most desperate of hopes: the contrary was more likely—a slower death by all the means imagined in a savage and unforgiving world. Better above all, doubtless reckoned the men of Warangal, that their families not die by a stranger's hand. If the survivors were not immediately massacred, then slavery and relocation always played a part in the defeat of a city. Indeed, the customs of war told the general and his troops that once a resisting city had been taken, no scruples of mercy were required. Every outrage against person and property was possible in the fullness of victory. This is how King Ashurnasipal dealt with one rebellious city and its leaders:

> In the valor of my heart and with the fury of my weapons I stormed the city.... I built a pillar over against ... [the] city gate, and I flayed all the chief men who had revolted, and I covered the pillar with their skins; some I walled up within the pillar, some I impaled upon the pillar on stakes, and others I bound to stakes round the pillar; many within the border of my own land I flayed, and I spread their skins upon the walls; and I cut off the limbs of the officers, of the royal officers who had rebelled. Ahiababa I took to Nineveh, I flayed him, I spread his skin upon the wall of Nineveh....[4]

Faced with the prospect of taking or defending a city, an army could always pray for a quick solution, but the uncertain consequences mitigated against a favorable outcome for the defeated. Soldiers defeated on a field of battle always had the choice of running—a choice almost never available in an invested city. Knowing full well that trapped soldiers fought harder, to the death if necessary, the ancient master of war Sun Tzu advised the general when attacking a city to provide for a "Golden Bridge," leaving one's enemy an avenue of escape as a last resort. Otherwise, wrote the Master Sun, "this is no strategy."[5]

All too often, however, strategy had less to do with city fighting than other, more fundamental objectives. In all likelihood, a survey of most sieges and assaults on cities would reveal how fast, militarily expedient operations are pushed aside by the passion for plunder or revenge or any number of other motives. Here is how one siege was consummated, just at the outbreak of the Peloponnesian War:

> ....when [the Plataeans] realized that the Thebans were inside their gates and that their city had been taken over in a moment, they were ready enough to come to an agreement.... But while negotiations were going on they became aware that the Thebans were not there in great force and came to the conclusion that, if they attacked them, they could easily overpower them.... They decided therefore that the attempt should be made, and, to avoid being seen going through the streets, they cut passages through the connecting walls of their houses and so gathered together in number. They made barricades by dragging wagons into the streets, and arranged everything else in the way that seemed likely to be most useful in their present position. When their preparations were as complete as could be, they waited for a time just before dawn, when it was still dark, and then sallied out from their houses against the Thebans. Their idea was that if they attacked in daylight their enemies would be more sure of themselves and would be able to meet them on equal terms, where in the night they would not be so confident and would also be at a disadvantage through

> not knowing the city so well as the Plataeans did. They therefore attacked at once, and fighting broke out immediately.
>
> As soon as the Thebans realized that they had fallen into a trap, they closed their ranks and fought back wherever they were attacked. Twice and three times they succeeded in beating off the [enemy but they eventually lost] heart and turned and fled through the city, most of them having no idea, in the darkness and the mud, on a moonless night at the end of the month, of which way to go in order to escape, while their pursuers knew quite well how to prevent them from escaping. The result was that most of them were destroyed.... Such was the fate of those who entered the town.[6]

This account of the siege of Plataea, given to us by Thucydides, is the single most detailed description of a siege up to this time. So, if Plataea is important to us because it has been written about so famously, as a city at war it was important enough to attract Thucydides' keen eye in the first place. There are things to be learned in Plataea.

Plataea was an ancient city, protected by 1,500 yards of wall, holding between 1,000 and 500 citizens. The town lay eight miles south of Thebes, the capital of Boetia, along the road to its ally Sparta. Plataea was in the Athenian camp.[7] This particular division of allegiances made Plataea important: the city thwarted the line of communications between Sparta and one of her most important allies.

The art of siegecraft in ancient Greece was certainly not the equal of that of the Persians, nor would their experience in this long war much improve it. Plataea appeared to be a formidable place to the Thebans, and so they decided to take the city by treachery, suborning certain anti-Athenian elements inside the city. At the proper time, in the dead of night, traitors would open the town's gates to an advance guard of 300 Thebans. The traitors hoped, of course, that their competitors would be killed in their sleep by the Thebans, but the Thebans would not go so far. Instead, the *fait accompli* they had planned for dawn, they thought, would prevent any resistance from breaking out. In modern terms, this action was to be a "decapitation."

The anti-Athenian traitors had seriously miscalculated. Because they were oligarchs, and thus despised the democratic party that held power in the town, they believed that killing just a few of the leaders would cause the entire city to surrender. But it appears that Plataea was more genuinely democratic than the anti-Athenians thought. When the Thebans refused to kill the city's leaders outright, the traitors were put in a very vulnerable position.

Before long, all the Thebans and their allies were vulnerable. The Thebans had assumed the whole business would be finished by dawn, which was when the main body of their army was to have arrived. But it rained. The main body was delayed. And that is when the population of the city mobilized against the invader, with the results duly noted by Thucydides. Perhaps half of the Theban advance guard survived for the moment. Later, they would all be executed, along with the Plataean traitors, too, one assumes.

The fate of the Thebans at Plataea underscores one of the abiding dangers of fighting in a city: the initiative, made even more tentative by a poorly conceived plan, slipped away from the Thebans during the night. The Theban advance guard may have entered the city as one, but they died one by one before the night ended.

Of course, the story does not end here. From then on, Plataea was in danger; it was now a place where revenge must be taken. Within two years, Archidamus, the king of Sparta, would stand outside the walls of Plataea with his army, and eventually Plataea would fall. None inside would survive.[8] Plataea, at least, enjoyed a momentary triumph. Most cities were not that fortunate.

Five hundred years and many sieges later, Roman legions fought one another at the northern Italian city of Cremona. The convoluted politics and internecine warfare in the "Year of the Four Emperors" need not concern us here. Suffice to say, it was easy to choose the wrong side and often just as dangerous to choose the right one. The art of siegecraft had advanced considerably; now cities were even less safe than they had been. And there were more cities. Taking and sacking cities—even large, well-defended ones like Cremona—had become more commonly a part of war. The fighting at Cremona would not have warranted even a footnote had the event not been recorded in some detail by none other than Tacitus.[9] It is this detail that permits us to see a premodern siege with extraordinary clarity.

Cremona had been established in 118 B.C. by Rome as one of its colonial towns along the Po River. Rome had settled 6,000 families here originally, but by the time of the civil war in 69 A.D., Cremona was a mature city with perhaps as many as 50,000 residents.[10] Toward the end of this particular year, the tides of war had washed up elements of as many as sixteen different legions, each professing allegiance to one warring faction or another. Several skirmishes and approach battles had brought legions loyal to Emperor Vespasian to the outskirts of the city. His commander on the spot, the veteran Antonius, implored his fatigued troops to rest before taking on Cremona.[11]

But his troops, having routed two rebel legions already, were in a riotous mood. The legions in these times were brittle instruments of power, ferocious on the field of battle when they were so inclined, mutinous when they were otherwise engaged. They elected their own commanders sometimes, and more often deposed them when they pleased.

Antonius' legions outside Cremona were in a hurry to capture the city before negotiations could ruin the chance for spoils: ". . . the soldiers have the plunder of a city that is stormed, the generals of one which capitulates," argued the soldiers. When one of their commanders tried to address them, the troops struck their weapons against their shields so that no one could hear him.[12]

In the end, Antonius' legionnaires took Cremona. Led by the eagles of the veteran 7th and 18th Legions, 40,000 of them broke into the city after heavy fighting. They were followed by 40,000 more in the form of camp followers, hangers-on, and contractors of one sort or another. The massacre lasted four days and proceeded with such abandon that all Italy was said to have reacted with shame. For months afterward, no one would buy slaves from Cremona.[13] For Tacitus, the explanation of the savagery lay in the tribal composition of the troops. "In an army which included such varieties of language and character, an army comprising Roman citizens, allies, and foreigners, there was every kind of lust, each man had a law of his own, and nothing was forbidden." Nothing but a shrine outside the city walls was left standing after the fight. "Such was the end of Cremona," Tacitus writes, "286 years after its foundation."[14] But Tacitus wrote Cremona's epitaph too soon. The Emperor Vespasian ordered the city rebuilt a few years later. In the seventh century, the city would be destroyed again, and again rebuilt. From the sixteenth through the nineteenth century, Cremona would change hands repeatedly. In 1990, the population of Cremona was more than 75,000.[15] Cities tend to persist.

Fortified towns and field armies battled with one another for supremacy all the way into the nineteenth century. When the invention of gunpowder blew away the old curtain walls of masonry in the fifteenth and sixteenth centuries, low-slung earthen bastions in star-shaped configurations—the *trace italienne*—became a genuine military fad. Being able to withstand the most powerful artillery of the day, the *trace italienne* extended the duration of sieges and made fortified cities anchors of a military world in which the defense was the stronger form of war. Towns—even small towns—mattered more than open-field battles. Battles could still be won, but they meant less, as one

A modern city of ancient Roman design, Palmanova, Italy

soldier saw at the time: "One good town well defended sufficeth to ruyn a mightie army." Experienced soldiers assumed that no fortified town of much consequence could be taken by any means other than a blockade. Starvation, not firepower or maneuver, held the balance of power in the warfare of the day.[16]

Those inside the city were not the only ones in danger of starvation, however. In one notorious siege from this time, those conducting the siege were less-well provisioned that those inside. The German city of Magdeburg had held out for nearly six months while the besiegers (an imperial army under Count Pappenheim) had stripped the surrounding countryside of sustenance. By May 1631, the nearest provisions were inside the city. When Magdeburg fell to a general assault, perhaps 20,000 or more of its 30,000 citizens were massacred. The laws of the siege had not changed in 2,000 years: Magdeburg was entirely at the mercy of its captors, and they showed none. Afterward, as usual, there was much insincere clucking about the barbarity of war, but this war would not abate for another seventeen years.[17]

For all practical purposes, the *trace italienne* was the last real fortification fad. Forts built as late as the nineteenth century were indistinguishable from their sixteenth century predecessors. Gradually, as cities grew in number and dimension, there arose the suspicion that it was possible for cities to become too big and too complicated to protect themselves by the traditional means of walled enclosure. Cities would be protected by battle, or not at all.

But that begged the question of where the battle for the city would be fought? When the Plataeans recalculated their chances, the enemy was already inside the gates. Having little choice, the Plataeans made the best of the advantages they had—including a knowledge of their own city, so intimate that they more easily could fight at night. So the battle, such as it was, played out in the dead of night, in the streets, alleyways, and (literally) dead-ends. When the enemy was finally able to concentrate his forces, the units were at about 50 percent of original strength, and the only options were surrender or a last stand.

As early as Aristotle, thinkers had considered the military advantages conferred by certain city designs, and street designs as well. Aristotle thought that irregularity worked to the defender's advantage, whereas regularity worked to the attacker's. Renaissance architects took up Aristotle's ideas anew. Ancient and irregular town patterns appealed not only to Leon Alberti's aesthetic sense but to his military sense as well, when he argued that "if an enemy comes into them he may be at a loss, and be in confusion and suspense; or if he pushes on daringly, may be easily destroyed."[18] Walls and other elaborate fortifications were expensive to build and maintain and served fewer and fewer practical functions as the years went on. If one assumed that the battle would be fought *inside* the city, one could integrate defensive functions with the city's design.

Napoleon III may have had this in mind when he commissioned the Baron Haussmann for the reconstruction of Paris in the mid-nineteenth century. Almost from the beginning, Paris' growth rate and growth patterns defied being confined to the existence of a mere military town. The town's first wall, enclosing the twenty acres of the *Ile de la Cité*, dated from A.D. 250. The next wall, built in the thirteenth century, was put up as much to watch over a newly enlarged market as for defense. The newest wall—the fifth system of fortification in its history—was put up in 1840-41, and again it was aimed at policing the inhabitants. In effect, Paris has always been defenseless against invaders, defenseless against internal disorder too.[19] When Baron Haussmann deftly isolated the most rebellious of the eastern neighborhoods by filling in a canal that had figured largely in the revolt of the June Days in 1848, Napoleon

III was ecstatic: now, said the emperor, faubourg St. Honoré could be taken from the rear.[20]

No city has ever been free from attack simply because it was fortified. What one would call the deterrent effect of fortifications seems to have always been slight. Despite its long career with walls and other fortifications, Paris has been a much besieged and often captured city. On the eve of the Franco-Prussian War of 1870, Paris had been besieged eight times since it suffered its first Viking raid in the ninth century.[21] So it seems somehow fitting that the siege of Paris in 1870-71 introduced the modern age of siege warfare.

That siege began in earnest after the German Army had routed the French in a series of field battles immediately after the outbreak of the war. By September, Napoleon III had been deposed by a popular uprising, mainly in Paris, his dictatorship replaced by a republic. While the German Third Army and the Army of the Meuse methodically surrounded Paris, the rest of the German army attended to Metz, where the remainder of the French army had concentrated.

General Helmuth von Moltke, the chief of the Prussian Great General Staff, never had any idea of storming Paris. He meant instead to bottle up the seething social unrest inside the city until the cork popped. It was a wonder that the French had not capitulated already. By all the standards of modern war, they should have: a national leader captured on the battlefield, a national government in flight, an army in disarray—any of these should have been sufficient reasons for surrender. To Moltke's surprise, and everyone else's, the French showed no signs of being reasonable. Before long, German lines of communication were under attack by French irregulars (the *francs-tireurs*), and inside Paris, General Louis Trochu, the nominal commander on the spot, was laying plans of a sort for a long and self-denying resistance. The defending garrison of Paris was optimistically counted as 400,000 men. Only one-fourth of these were regular soldiers of the French Army. The rest were a hodge-podge that included the highly combustible "republican" force, the *garde nationale*, armed civilians of various political coloration, and no small number of refugees who had been displaced by the German advances—all in all, a mixture that always seemed on the verge of riot and mutiny and sometimes crossed the line.[22] The putative *chef d'etat*, Leon Gambetta, had escaped the city by balloon and hoped to organize national resistance from Tours. Throughout the ordeal, however, the question persisted: who could say authoritatively for France that France was ready to negotiate?

What was beyond question, at least for the Germans, was that this war would be decided by negotiation, not by battle. General Trochu wanted to lure the Germans into the city itself in order to create, he said—referring to the quagmire that had entrapped Napoleon's forces in Spain earlier in the century"—another Saragossa." No one on the German side was having any of that, from the crown prince on down the chain of command. The siege was already a month old when the Prince gave his opinion on whether the city would be taken by *force majeur*: "All persons in authority, I at the head of them, are at one in this, that we must use every endeavour to force Paris to surrender by hunger alone."[23]

As time passed, it became clear that hunger would take too long. No one in the German high command seemed enthusiastic about the prospect of bombardment, but perhaps it would hurry things along. A leading officer of the staff, Bronsart von Schellendorf, was adamantly opposed. Bombardment had already been tried at Strasbourg, he argued, and that had just wasted ammunition, turned the civil population against them, and had not brought surrender one day closer.[24] All the same, on the grounds of "attacking the morale" of the Parisians, the Germans turned on the guns just after the new year began. No strictly military reason for this could be found. Inside the city, rations were low and starvation was threatening by the end of the year, but time, the German high command believed, was against them.

The bombardment of Paris lasted the better part of a month, with shells coming in at the rate of three to four hundred a day, causing little damage but doing much to improve morale—French morale. While the guns were going, General Trochu managed to mount several attacks against the German siege lines but to little avail. All around Paris, in the provinces, remnants of the French army and irregulars were in more or less constant action against the German main bodies and their lines of communication. None had a chance of rescuing Paris by breaking the siege, much less of reversing the German success, but these operations worked to the advantage of French morale and the detriment of German official will. The longer the war dragged on, the more European opinion turned against Germany and in favor of France. Among modern nations at arms, morale seemed to count for more than battlefield results; indeed, it almost seemed that France was staying in this war by force of morale alone.[25]

In the end, however, General von Moltke was right: winning the old way, on the battlefield itself, was beyond the reach of armies under the conditions of modern warfare. Now, the purpose of an army was to create the conditions in which the objectives of the war could be won at the tables of diplomacy. In late January, an armistice was declared, and on 1 March 1871, German troops marched into Paris.[26]

The siege of Paris was not important merely because it was peculiar—which, compared to earlier sieges, it was—but because it was more like those sieges that followed it. In important respects, the siege of Paris was the first of the modern sieges, for sieges in the twentieth century were going to take on some unique characteristics.[27]

The Typology of a Siege

The fundamental design of the classic siege had long since been formed during the wars of antiquity, and it was a design that would not be substantially changed until the twentieth century. Even today, though in modern uniform, the classic siege is easily recognizable. Viewed from the perspective of the offense, the siege is composed of several stages, stages that are progressive and sequential—if all goes well for the attacking force:

- The Approach
- The Investment
- The Preparation
- The Assault
- The "Dog Fight"
- Domination and Occupation
- Withdrawal.

The approach to a siege belongs as much to the realm of strategy and operations as any other aspect of siegecraft. Whether an army deliberately intends to lay siege to a city as part of a general campaign—as in the case of Plataea—or whether actions on the battlefield develop in such a way as to require an attack on a city will influence what happens next. An army that had no intention of besieging a city—as in the case of Cremona—will see, once faced with the prospect, that an army is not automatically prepared to conduct operations against a city that means to defend itself.

How elaborate the next stage, the investment, will be again depends upon the operational intent of the attacking army and whether the city in question is the point of the campaign or is beside the point. The length of time and the amount of energy invested in this stage could be as little as a few hours or as long as several months. The nature of the investment depends also upon whether or not the attacking army is opposed by an enemy field army and whether that army is bound to attack the besiegers directly or whether they are content to remain a vague threat, just beyond the horizon. It was for this reason, early in the history of siegecraft, that commanders and their field engineers learned the art of protecting their own positions while laying down entrenchments to encircle the besieged city—techniques known as circumvallation and countervallation.

Once the city was more or less invested, quarantined from any sort of relief, another decision awaited the besieging commander. Should the city be starved into submission or be taken by main force? As we have seen, this decision is not always a straightforward one for the commander to make. The operational and tactical momentum of the attacking force might carry it promptly against the city's defenses with little or no preparation so that the elapsed time of the siege proper was only a few hours. On the other hand, the record is replete with armies that were more than happy to settle down in their siege lines, building what amounted to a kind of mirror city to watch over the city under siege.

If the city falls of its own weight, by means of treachery or because of the hardships of those trapped inside the city, no assault is required, and the besieging troops will enter the city in a triumphal march. In any such situation, no doubt some citizens of the city will acquiesce to the occupation, while others will not, and what form resistance—if any—takes will be determined in large measure by the division of sentiments. The occupation may be a quiet or a riotous one. In this case, if there is fighting to be done, this is the stage at which it will break out.

Besieging armies commonly lose more casualties during the investment and preparation phases than any other. The enforced immobility, the generally wretched conditions in the siege lines, and the tactical disadvantage of having an enemy always on the "high ground"—all combine to test the besieging army as severely as any test by combat. After the improvements in fortification design necessitated by the appearance of gunpowder, aggressive circumvallation (the gradual tightening of the investing lines) in the preparatory phase became harder and more dangerous than ever before. Besieging armies mined approaches more confidently as well, and trenches took forms that we recognize today. The stages of investment and preparation were the most difficult thus far for a besieging army and were usually the point at which armies gave up their sieges or in which sieges were broken by relieving armies.

The preparations completed, the timing and method of assault are determined by the immediate tactical circumstances, including the design of the fortification under siege. The immediate objective of the assault, of course, is the breaching of the wall, and more than once, armies have failed here. Repeated assaults are not at all unusual in siege warfare, and it is at the wall that the power of the two combatants find their fullest expression, where victory or defeat is found in classical siege warfare. A successful *escalade*, in fact, is the main objective of any besieging army in the classical way of siegecraft. There are, indeed, subsequent stages, as shall be seen, but these have less to do with the winning of victory than the consequences of it.

A successful breach of a defended wall did not necessarily signal an end to the fighting. The "Dog Fight" consists of minor tactics at their most intense, perhaps as intense a form of combat as any, with the possible exception of jungle combat. Undirected and uncontrolled street fighting might well go on for days after the enemy has penetrated the city. Here, too, the siege is often transformed into a quite different form of action. Here is where the looting, plundering, and wanton violence are most likely to be found. Indeed, it is more than possible that in the history of siege warfare, more inhabitants of the city have been killed here than at any other stage. As we have seen, massacres are sometimes inadvertent, unplanned results of the frenzies generated by hard fighting. Sometimes, of course, commanders simply have no control over troops after they break through city defenses. Sometimes, massacres of cities are planned from the outset of the campaign, when the object is annihilation.

As with the other stages, the nature of the occupation and the withdrawal take their cue from the nature of the operations that preceded them. Occupations can run the gamut from the benign to the savage, and often within the same war, the same army can adopt very different policies: the German occupations of Paris and Warsaw during World War II would never be confused with one another, for instance. By the same token, one might think an army always withdraws voluntarily from a city it has occupied, but there is more than one way to leave a city: one army can be ejected by another. In World War II, this process was often referred to as a "liberation," a highly dubious term subject to considerable interpretation, as when the Imperial Japanese Army "liberated" the Chinese city of Nanking at the cost of more than 200,000 noncombatant casualties.

From the point of view of the defense, that is from the view of the city itself, modern developments have been most unkind. For the longest time, cities had been capable of defending themselves. On the approach of an enemy, a city might raise an army from its own reservoir of manpower and launch a preemptive attack in open field battle, well away from the city. In fact, this, not a classical siege, is what happened at the Troy of legend and history. Or if it proved impossible to keep the enemy at arm's length, a city might defend itself on the walls. There, the defenders enjoyed the advantages of superior observation, force protection, and even what would come to be called "interior lines," since defenders could always rush from one point to another faster than their enemies. If the city was well provisioned, the defenders along the walls had the advantage of immediate support of all kinds and categories. And finally, in the age of manpower-intensive warfare, it was clear that fewer men were required to defend a city than were required to take it—by a ratio of at least 1 to 3.

But as the Plataeans showed as well as anyone, even if defenders lost the battle of the walls, it was not a foregone conclusion that the day was lost. Exhausted attackers could be lulled by their success at the wall into thinking—hoping—that their battles were over. Perhaps the victory at the wall was followed by a period of quiet, in which the conquered inhabitants might appear to be acquiescent. Indeed, there might be a significant lapse of time between the apparent victory and the outbreak of the Dog Fight. The lapse of time might be such that the original army had been replaced by administrators, come to manage an easy occupation. The outbreak of resistance then takes on something of the nature of a revolt or uprising, with all the tactical advantages and disadvantages accruing to this form of action.

This uprising could conceivably lead to forcing the enemy to withdraw summarily, but there are many more cases in which the withdrawal is ordered because military fortunes elsewhere have turned against the original attacker. In the sixteenth century, particularly in the Low Countries, there were many cases in which relief armies invested the original besiegers or forced a retirement by means of an open-field battle. This was exactly the threat that General von Moltke faced when he tightened his siege lines around Paris nearly three hundred years later.

The Modern Siege

The same social and technical advancements that altered the face of modern warfare in general changed the art of the siege as well. The advancements did not so much change the nature of warfare as how that nature would manifest itself. The commonest principles, values, and actions of war took on different meanings after the nineteenth century and often manifested themselves differently than before. The simplest of factors, that of scale, changed so radically that its effects reverberated throughout the whole art of war. Under the new regimes of the nations-at-arms after the French Revolution, the whole idea of "mass" had to be thought of differently. "Mass" became not merely of local value but of operational and strategic value as well. And, so, a geography of battle that had not changed since antiquity was redrawn, extending the reach of war beyond the narrow tactical confines of old toward a truly global reach, with weapons and military technology to match.

Not surprisingly, the geography of the siege would change along with these larger developments. Armies grew, and the space they required to function grew as well, and when such armies met, the space consumed by their actions was several magnitudes greater than the space taken up by previous battles. In the same way, whereas forces conducting the siege once operated within close proximity to their objective, in the twentieth century, the tyranny of physical mass—the necessity for big numbers to do big things in war—began to lose its power. From the First World War onward, the instruments of force dispersed, even as their application focused more precisely on its objective. In this paradoxical development, no technical factor was so dramatic in its effect as the airplane. Beginning with its introduction in the First World War, the old assumption that weapons must be massed in order to mass their effects would be gradually less and less tenable.

The Aerial Siege

Within one decade of the airplane's debut as a weapon of war, military theorists were imagining how a war might be won by means of air power alone. Even though the airplane was still technologically crude, little effort was required to conjure up scenarios in which an entire nation might be subdued by means of aerial warfare alone.[28] The only question was when technological developments could execute what the early theorists had imagined. By 1940, the divide between technology and theory seemed to have narrowed sufficiently to produce what had long been promised, and London, the world's largest city, was about to become the world's largest target. The first aerial siege in history—and one of the longest—was about to begin.[29]

When 900 German aircraft launched their first raids on London in September 1940, there was already a small store of experience ready to comfort the skeptical, if any could be found in Nazi Germany by then. Earlier that year, the *Luftwaffe* had staged a raid on the Dutch port of Rotterdam, and although this operation could not be classed a siege, the actual destruction and the psychological effect of the raid were sufficient to encourage a Dutch surrender. Nearly a thousand citizens were killed, and 20,000 buildings destroyed. No doubt the Rotterdam raid was inspired by the results of the *Luftwaffe's* attack on Warsaw during the Germans' offensive the previous year. In those operations, however, the German High Command did not expect that any sort of decision would be won as a result of air action alone. The air siege against Great Britain, and London, in particular, was to be a different matter. If Warsaw and Rotterdam were more properly operations in support of ground offensives, there was the expectation that the Battle of Britain would be fought and won or lost in the air entirely, after which a seaborne invasion would consummate the victory already won.

The German High Command did not come around to this concept right away. The air siege of London and its counterpart against Berlin and the other German cities were stumbled into by a series of escalating reprisals following an accidental bombing of London. Reprisals were quickly transformed into national policy, and the air war against the cities of Germany began in earnest by early September 1940.

Throughout the interwar years, military theorists, strategists, and war planners had been fed a steady diet of optimistic forecasts on the effect of aerial bombardment on defenseless civilians, forecasts that were based as much upon an uncomplimentary view of civilians as on technological realities. And during these years, a few aerial operations—such as those of the German Condor Legion during the Spanish Civil War—had contributed to the optimism. The celebrated destruction of the Spanish city of Guernica may have been occasion for a humanitarian outcry in some quarters, but aviators saw in Guernica a ray of hope that cities could be brought to their knees solely by means of air attack.[30]

London would check this untested optimism. For five weeks, the *Luftwaffe* dropped about one hundred tons of explosives on London every night. In all, the Germans flew 12,000 sorties over the city. Far from ceasing to function as a city, London and Londoners quickly adapted to even the most destructive raids, day or night. On both sides of the siege, what quickly became apparent was the great distance between predictions and actual experience under fire.[31]

Before the war, the British Ministry of Health had forecasted 20,000 to 30,000 dead on the first night of a massive aerial bombardment, eventually reaching a total of 600,000 killed and 1,200,000 more casualties during a hypothetical war. In April 1939, the Ministry of Health had sent local officials one million burial forms and half a million papier-mâche coffins. Expecting three times as many psychiatric casualties as those physically wounded, London hospitals organized a triage plan and added 10,000 more beds to accommodate surges in casualties.[32] These preparations proved to be overdrawn. The first attacks produced 300 casualties. Refugees from the East End did need relocation assistance, but they were not the thousands of hysterics, traumatized by the bombs that had been feared.

Other forecasts were equally mistaken: gas was expected to play a leading role in aerial attacks, but in the event, the greatest problems were fire and unexploded bombs, both of which hampered the mobility of emergency services and public traffic. Even at the height of the raids, in mid-September, one million people came into the city to work. As time passed, the raids became less episodic and more nearly constant. Deep underground shelters had not been provided for, however, and in this case, the Londoners found a ready and practical solution: a subway ticket, which admitted one to the relative safety of the underground "Tube" stations. Sensibly, officials began improving seventy-nine stations to accommodate several tens of thousands of people, night and day. The usual number taking shelter nightly was estimated at 100,000 people. Even with the Tube stations running more or less smoothly, estimates were that 60 percent of Londoners still slept at home.[33] Interpreting the progress of the aerial siege as generously as he could, Hitler was heard to hope that "Britain might yet be seized by mass hysteria." In fact, the number of hospitalized mentally ill actually declined.[34]

The gap between expectation and reality closed in early October, when Hitler finally ordered the cancellation of invasion plans. The *Luftwaffe*, driven by Goring, continued to hold out the possibility that London might be defeated by unceasing night raids, although Goring seems to have had no factual basis for his optimism. The siege continued at varying degrees of intensity until early May 1941. London's fundamental cohesion, the city's capacity to function as a highly integrated metropolis, was not irreparably damaged by the German air campaign for one reason: physical destruction was not the same as systems destruction. The infrastructure of urban support systems—public order, power, water, medical facilities, emergency services, public transport—never collapsed. All the fatuous predictions of social disintegration were proved wrong—and wrongheaded.

But Allied bombers were sent against German and Japanese cities with the same objectives in mind, that somehow enemy morale could be moved to work in favor of Allied aims. For all that London and other British cities had suffered during the Blitz, German and Japanese cities suffered much worse. By one accounting, 79 percent of Bremerhaven was destroyed by Allied bombing; 75 percent of Hamburg; Kiel, 69 percent; Munster, 65 percent. Numerous other major German cities were 50 percent destroyed. In such company as this, Berlin, with 33 percent destroyed, seems fortunate.[35] By the end of the air campaign against Japan in the spring of 1945, fully 60 percent of the civilian population of Japan had left their cities and were trying to live in the countryside—but what of the 40 percent who did not leave the cities? Tokyo suffered the single most destructive aerial attack of the war, in which more than 83,000 were killed and more than fifteen square miles of the city center destroyed, but the city continued to function and was functioning after a fashion when Allied occupation forces arrived.[36] In all of World War II, no city was ever completely subdued by air attack to the point of breakdown—even Hiroshima and Nagasaki.

Was it possible to kill a town? Yes, so long as it was not too big or complex. In retaliation for the assassination of Nazi Governor Reinhard Heydrich by Czech partisans in 1942, Hitler chose the village of Lidice for a Carthagenian-style eradication. All of the nearly 500 residents were either executed immediately (199 men), deported to concentration camps (198 women), or sent to prison orphanages (98 children). Lidice was a small village, but the effort to kill it was not small. The whole site was bulldozed, a nearby river was rerouted, and what remained was "landscaped" to erase any trace of its existence. No military advantage whatever accrued from Lidice's murder. The destruction of the village was not an act of war but an act of policy.[37]

But as we have seen, the great combatant cities of World War II had advantages that a village like Lidice did not enjoy. First, sheer size enters into the matter. London, Berlin, Tokyo—all these were simply too large for the weapons of the day to bring down. The worst of the air raids on London and Tokyo focused on the center of the city, yet even with the substantial destruction suffered by both—Tokyo's far worse than London's—only a small part of the whole metropolis was affected in each case. Second, the complexity factor demonstrated that it had a real military effect, for urban complexity was clearly bound up with urban redundancy: those who were organized into London fire brigades were well placed to assist in the location and disposal of unexploded bombs, a function that had no real peacetime counterpart. Those who were organized to run the London Underground system were well placed to assist in providing for the tens of thousands who sought refuge during the night raids. Any city so accustomed to moving large numbers of people every day, as all these cities were, would not easily be prevented from continuing to do so by the partial destruction of one small part of a transport system: in London's case, one million workers commuted *into* London every day during the German blitz. At the same time, two million Londoners decided for themselves that they would evacuate the city, but this was done so gradually and without difficulty that few noticed at first. Before the war, the expectation was that at the beginning of aerial attacks, the roadways and subways would be choked with hysterical refugees. After Hitler canceled the invasion in October, the battle of London was no longer a siege but a punitive operation—no different in kind, surely, from the operation against Lidice—and no more effective in the end. Without hope of winning a victory, the *Luftwaffe* was a means without an end.

"A Continuation of Policy by Other Means"

The lack of proportion between military commitment and military result that became obvious to General von Moltke during the siege of Paris was to be duplicated many times over in the twentieth century. But what Moltke saw at Paris in 1870 was not a novel development in war making. Paris, a national symbol in peace, served the same role in time of war. The city was not simply another place on the map: its importance transcended any of its physical attributes, its political or economic or even its military value. One might even say Paris was—and is—a spiritually critical element of France. Not many places can claim this sort of spiritual importance. Merely being a capital city is not quite enough to excite such depths of feeling. Few Americans could ever have been accused of feeling so strongly about their national capital or, indeed, about any of their cities.

Before 1916, the town of Verdun could hardly be said to have been one of these places, although it certainly had a history as one of France's frontier forts since the ninth century.[38] But this place, above all others on the trace lines of the Western Front of World War I, purchased a new, intensely spiritual identity in that year. That was when both Germany and France invested this old fortified town with strategic importance and, in the process, made the siege of Verdun one of the most famous sieges of the twentieth century. Chief of the German General Staff

Erich von Falkenhayn's deliberate use of the siege for strategic ends is of particular interest here.

By the end of 1915, Falkenhayn had concluded that Germany could not win the war on the battlefield. In his eyes, Great Britain was the centerpiece of all Allied power, and it was beyond the reach of Germany's power. The only possible way for Germany to get at all-important British power was by attacking the alliance itself, and this he meant to do by crafting a new strategy that, in effect, would separate France from the allies by convincing the French that "in a military sense they have nothing more to hope for."[39] The technique Falkenhayn chose for the execution of his strategy was an old one, known even to the ancient Greeks as *epiteichismos*: attacking a place so valuable to the enemy that he is obliged to defend it. Verdun was important only because it would elicit the reaction from the French that Falkenhayn desired.

Falkenhayn depended upon the French to defend Verdun at all costs. It was essential that they should, for his strategic objective was to use the battle to pile up so many casualties that France would sue for a separate peace. It was a strategy designed, as one scholar has written, "to turn the domestic flank of France...."[40] And it might win the war: if France were to sue for a separate peace, Great Britain would have no choice, then being isolated, but to do likewise.

The town of Verdun proper was only the garrison town and anchor for a larger region that in early 1916 formed a salient along the front-line trace. The operation against Verdun was planned in such a way that, if the strategic ends were achieved, tactical objectives would automatically be taken care of along the way. On 21 February, after an intense bombardment, the German Fifth Army assaulted along an eight-mile-wide front. Of course, the French counterattacked, retaking a few of the early German gains in ground. The Germans retaliated, and so the grind began. From February to December, defending or attacking Verdun was the main effort of the German and French armies. By the close of the campaign, the siege had consumed nearly one million casualties. The original trace of the front lines had changed very little. The Allies were not so close to defeat as Falkenhayn had assumed. Verdun did not drive a wedge between them, even after the equally disastrous Allied offensive on the Somme began in the summer.[41] Verdun was not war so much as militarized policy; indeed, it is difficult to disagree with the assessment of one informed analyst:

> The questionable strategy of pounding the enemy to the negotiation table was matched with operational plans that did not fit the strategic goal, and was executed with tactics that were self-defeating. The battle was fought in the most traditional manner of nineteenth-century offensive land warfare at a point of attack where the old guard of professional strategists would have avoided battle at all costs. . . . More than any other battle, Verdun showed the military impasse of World War I, the complete disjuncture between strategy, battle design, and tactics, and the inability to use the modern means of war.[42]

Armed with the tools of the Industrial Revolution, the combatants of Verdun took ten months to produce nearly one million casualties—among them, 600,000 killed. No one on either side pretended for a moment that Verdun or even the operational area it anchored was worth this price, especially before the battle commenced. Later in the battle, naturally, the casualties already suffered were invoked by both sides as a way of ennobling even more sacrifices in advance, but there was a sort of weight-bearing limit of such rhetoric—as the great mutinies of 1917 would show. Whatever value Verdun might have had was merely a product of what the combatants themselves invested in it.

Verdun was chosen quite deliberately to act as a theater-level slaughterhouse. But it is easy enough to find considerable towns or cities in history that were enlisted, so to speak, for a strategic or operational purpose, not because they had any intrinsic quality worth defending to the last soldier.

Stalingrad was one such place. The Second World War battle that now epitomizes the modern siege was fought over a city that was certainly no crown jewel in anyone's empire. The battle lasted from the end of August 1942, until the end of January 1943, and before it was over, Stalingrad and its immediate surroundings would attract well over a million soldiers, fighting for or against the city, or, perhaps in the end, fighting only for their own survival.

Stalingrad was also unplanned. One could not say that it was selected as an element in a broad strategic and operational scheme by one national military staff or the other. It was not. When the Germans and the Russians began their calculations for the summer campaigning season, neither assigned much military importance to this Volga River town. The major question facing the German High Command was where on the vast Eastern Front the army's main effort should be fixed.[43] As for the Russians, the major problem was how to combat what the Germans finally decided, for in the early summer of 1942, the

Photograph not available.

This picture was taken between 23 and 29 August 1942 by a group of Soviet military cameramen headed by V. Orlyankin during the mass bombardment of Stalingrad undertaken by the 4th German Air Fleet commanded by Rikhtgoffen. At that time the Soviet troops were retreating toward Stalingrad from the west.

Germans still had the strategic and operational initiative on the Eastern Front.

And that is how the summer began: the German armies resumed their offensives in May and rapidly created a new geography of the front. Retreating elements of the Soviet army and advance elements of the German army drew toward Stalingrad. By July, Stalingrad had come to be visualized as the anchor of two German army groups swinging southeastward for the Caucasus. For the Russians, Stalingrad had become the center of a line of national defense stretching from the Baltic to the Black Sea.[44]

Much was made, then and later, of Stalingrad's "central position," as if centrality itself conferred some positive military value upon a place. A central point also divides parts, and in this case, that is what happened on both sides. For the Germans, Stalingrad lay on the seam between Sixth Army and Fourth Panzer Army. Two Russian armies likewise divided—literally—at Stalingrad: the 62d Army held everything in the sector north of the Tsaritsa gorge, while the 64th held everything south of it. Stalingrad's "central position" belongs in the same category as the "guards the gate to the steppes" argument or "guards the Volga River line" argument. Cities no longer were capable of guarding river lines or steppes or anything else under conditions of modern industrial war. Not even themselves.[45]

Eventually both nations and their leaders convinced themselves that Stalingrad was a place of paramount importance. The Russians were not going to give up the city, whatever the cost, and the Germans were resolved to take it from them, whatever the cost. All summer long, forces seemed to converge upon Stalingrad as if drawn by a magnet. The more Hitler was disappointed by the slow progress of his forces toward the Caucasus, the more he fixated upon Stalingrad. Success here could compensate for shortcomings elsewhere. Stalin—for his part, equally intransigent—made withdrawal from Stalingrad tantamount to a crime against the Soviet state.[46]

If Stalingrad had no intrinsic strategic or operational value as a place neither contributing to nor detracting from strategic or operational objectives—one might well ask what the armies were doing there in the first place, fighting a form of war so far removed from the doctrines these armies had imagined for themselves. One can only note the result: few places if any concentrated as many combatant forces in such close proximity to one another as at Stalingrad. One way or another, the city had become an excellent place for the killing of large numbers of the enemy, and both sides saw the potential value of the situation.

The commitment to fight *à outrance* at Stalingrad had been made by both sides by the end of July. That done, the city seemed to promise another advantage to the combatants: it attracted and fixed in place units that would not otherwise be there. Both the Germans and the Russians came round to the idea, at different times, that Stalingrad could serve as a pivot on which to maneuver huge offensive operations. Hitler saw this possibility during the early summer, when he was apportioning forces for the coming offensives. The Russians came to the idea later, when it was clear that the Germans' operational maneuverability was impaired by the commitment they had made at Stalingrad. Then the Stavka planned several operations, one of them the successful Operation Uranus, that actually did the work of victory by cutting off the Sixth Army and trapping it in a pocket.

The city was long and narrow, befitting its location: its population of 500,000 spread itself almost thirty miles along the western bank of the Volga, but edges of the city were rarely more than 4,000-meters wide and sometimes as narrow as 1,500 meters. Only three terrain features of any significance were noted on the tactical maps: the river bank, which was high enough in places to afford some protection for troops just landed; the river Tsaritsa, which bisected the city; and the *Mamayet*

Kurgan, an old Tartar burial mount some 102-meters high. In the southern half of the city, only a massive concrete grain elevator stood out.[47]

The city possessed other, special tactical attributes, not the sort usually noted on standard military maps. Strung out, one after another, for five miles north from Mamayet Kurgan were four massive factories and their surrounding complexes. The first of these was the Lazure Chemical Plant. Slightly north of that came the Red October metal works, which was followed in turn by the *Barrikady* weapons plant and, finally, the Stalingrad Tractor Factory, which had long been converted to tank production.[48]

By the end of August, there were good reasons for the Russians to leave Stalingrad. Russia's 62d Army counted only 20,000 soldiers at the time. The 62d had retreated into the city, herded eastward by the Sixth Army's advance across the Don River. Just as it took refuge inside Stalingrad, the 62d would be assigned a new commander. Sixth Army was then in the business of becoming the single largest formation of the entire *Wehrmacht*, with a strength approaching one-third of a million men. Its commander, General Friedrich Paulus, estimated that his army would need ten days to take the city and then fourteen days to regroup and cross the Volga to the steppes beyond.[49]

The main body of the German offensive jumped off early in the morning of 24 August. Starting from its lodgment on the eastern banks of the Don River, 16th Panzer Division meant to race the thirty-five miles between the Don and Volga River and capture Stalingrad by coup de main. The night before, elements of the 79th Panzer Grenadier Regiment had made their way to the Volga, digging in along the river near the northern suburb of Spartanovka. All day long, the German advance was covered by the *Luftwaffe's* 8th Air Army, part of *Luftflotte IV*, which also staged saturation raids against the city. By the end of the first day, much of Stalingrad was wrecked. The systems for sewage treatment and water and much of the power were destroyed by the bombing, although somehow the power station in the southern part of the city managed to continue operating. The main hospital and all the major factory complexes suffered numerous direct hits. The streets were already full of rubble, and those inhabitants who could still function began burrowing into any protection they could find. Because Stalin had initially refused to let the citizens of the city evacuate, civilian casualties were already high. Stalin insisted, however, that the local militiamen would fight that much harder if they knew their fellow citizens were still in the city.[50]

Neither side had committed wholeheartedly to the idea of fighting to the last man for this city. For the Germans, Stalingrad was only a way point at the moment, a river town marking the boundary between the southernmost of their army groups and those in the north. The almost casual manner in which the city became important is belied by the speed with which it became important. Each side began to see in Stalingrad what they had not seen before—a place where one could do important damage to the enemy. Within two weeks of first contact, both sides had made their commitment, and the buildup began. By early October, the Germans had nine divisions in the area, some 90,000 men in all, with 2,000 guns, 300 tanks, with about 1,000 aircraft in support. At the same time, inside Stalingrad, the Russians had 55,000 men, supported by 950 guns and 500 mortars, 80 tanks, and about 180 aircraft.[51] Only by early December did Sixth Army reach its uppermost strength; the Sixth Army's *Quartiermeister* reported a ration strength of 275,000 men.[52]

The German troops that had collected at Stalingrad, it should be emphasized, were troops that could not be employed elsewhere. For the Russians to succeed, all that was required was to keep as many German troops tied up at Stalingrad as possible. Over a quarter of a million troops sounds like success. In the meantime, the Russians were able to assemble more than a million troops for their December counteroffensive, Operation Uranus. The effect of Uranus would be to cut 6th Army's lines of communication and thereby isolate it from the sustenance of the whole German army. Not for the first time was a besieger himself besieged, and at the end of January 1943, the Germans remaining in the Stalingrad pocket surrendered.

Of all the battles of the Second World War, Stalingrad was one of the most decisive. The battle produced results, permanent results, that Russia could not have achieved elsewhere at the time. The Germans' defeat here impaired their capacity to prosecute the war as they preferred and challenged their material and psychological balance. No less important, the defeat called into question Hitler's strategic wisdom even more seriously than had the defeat of the *Luftwaffe* over Great Britain.

For sheer scale of destructive savagery, few modern battles could match that of Stalingrad. Some writers have seen a new form of warfare emerging from the rubble and cellars of this battle.[53] Of course, it was not so new after all, but it was special, and it certainly was new to those who fought there (as it is always true that battle itself is new at some point to those who fight in them). In the half-light between knowledge and experience, the truth of the matter sometimes goes astray, that's all.

Stalingrad's inherent drama is so intense that it impaired judgment then and still does.

Stalingrad was certainly a siege but not a particularly well-conducted one, as sieges go. At no time was Stalingrad ever completely isolated. The city's line of communication to the rear was tenuous, always in danger. But it was never closed. In this respect, the Volga River was a very real asset for the defense. The river posed enough of a barrier to discourage adventurous enemy sorties, but not such a barrier that it could not be crossed by its defenders. Beyond the river, the village of Krasnaya Sloboda functioned as an immediate rear support area and fire base. This is where General Vasili Chuikov's 62d Army kept its heavy guns—to its credit and to its benefit. Simply finding a place in the city proper for gun lines, not to mention protecting them, were problems solved by the river. Chuikov was smart enough—and tough enough—to refuse when his artillery commander begged him to allow the gunners to fight alongside the men.

So, there was the lifeline across the river that could not be—or was not—cut. On the eve of one of the largest German assaults, *Luftflotte IV* was flying 3,000 sorties a day over Stalingrad. How many sorties were directed toward the river crossings and Krasnaya Sloboda and everything else that moved on the east side of the river is not known. Accounts agree that the *Luftwaffe* concentrated on direct support for the troops in the city proper, although even the pilots themselves wondered at the good that was being done by repeatedly bombing rubble.[54] By this time, Stalingrad had been *Luftflotte IV's* primary mission for more than six weeks.

The Red Army fired more ammunition in the battle of Stalingrad than in any other operation of the war.[55] Part of this dubious record derives from the sheer length of the siege. The siege of Leningrad was longer, but it was a classic investment, like the siege of Paris, in which the assailants did most of the shooting, but never broke into the city proper. The enemy broke into Stalingrad right away, established lines of investment, and sortied at will into the city. The Germans rarely had much difficulty getting into Stalingrad; staying there was the problem.

The difference between the two sieges is telling. Stalingrad was part of an operational plan that aimed to project German power well beyond the Volga. From the German perspective, a secure Stalingrad was important, perhaps even critical. At Leningrad, the prospects for a follow-on offensive after the siege were a good deal more problematic. Hitler's ambition to cut the Soviet line of communications from Murmansk-Archangel could not compare as a strategic priority with the

Caucasus oil fields—although perhaps it should have. Leningrad and Stalingrad looked different because, among other reasons, of what each side needed from victory.

"The Prestige Objective"

The interaction between strategic ends and means is no more obscure when cities are concerned than in any other form of warfare. Sometimes, this interaction is much faster, more intense, and more immediate than it might be if a city were not involved. The battle for Berlin in early 1945 illustrates this interaction as few other city battles could.

Some questioned whether there should be a battle for Berlin at all. The British were interested in taking the city and were not timid about saying so. Prime Minister Churchill pressed General Eisenhower and anyone else who would listen about Berlin's importance as a prize. General Montgomery did the same. The Soviets, too, wanted the city badly, but were not about to reveal their intentions too soon—even to the point of lying about it. On 1 April, Stalin cabled Eisenhower that the Soviet Union was not particularly interested in Berlin and considered the city a secondary target for his advancing armies.[56] Eisenhower was happy to let the Soviets have the "honor" of taking Berlin, if they wanted it; he did not see in a US effort to reduce the city any value that would outweigh the 100,000 casualties that it was estimated such an operation would incur. The British and the Soviets saw the taking of Berlin as the consummating act of the European war, while the Americans thought the destruction of the German armed forces would lead to the ultimate surrender of Berlin and every other city not yet occupied by the Allies. To the Americans, Berlin was a "prestige objective," not a military one.[57] To the British, Berlin was a prestige objective, too, but worth the effort to seize before the Soviets did. Eisenhower, however, would not agree with Montgomery's request for extra divisions so the British field marshal could try his hand against the city. Allowing for troops to be taken from the present lines to be used against Berlin might weaken the advance and place American troops at risk. The Soviets—in the person of Joseph Stalin—were not interested in being conservative where Germans were concerned, then or later. On the day when he denied being much interested in Berlin, the Soviet dictator ordered the date for the attack on Berlin: 16 April. Inside Berlin, the code name for commencement of this inevitable Soviet attack was "Clausewitz."[58]

When 1945 began, Berlin's population was estimated at 2.5 million people. Between the first of the year and March, however, the city suffered through no fewer than eleven massive air raids, driving perhaps as many as 200,000 people out. But to where? Soviet army advances were driving ever-larger streams of refugees toward Berlin and other western cities so that during the time when so many Berliners were supposed to have left, another half a million arrived in the city. About two million of Berlin's population, it was said, were women.[59]

The city proper covered 321 square miles and was bisected by the river Spree, which intercepted the river Havel in the western districts. From the southeast to the northwest, central precincts of the city were further divided by canals. The most important of the canals at the time, the Teltow, bypassed the center of the city and connected the Havel and the Spree. The canal formed a natural line of defense in the southern half of the city. The *Tiergarten* was the physical epicenter of the city, a great park laid on an east-west axis, fed into by the great *Unter den Linden* avenue, which was itself fronted by most of the important political and military headquarters. This district was the lair of the beast, as one Soviet officer put it. Only here could the beast be killed.

The lair was unprotected until late. Hitler would not countenance talk of fortifying Berlin until February, when the Soviets crossed the Oder-Neisse River line.[60] For the next three months, the rhetoric of denial clashed with ever-more insistent realities. The illustrated weekly *Das Reich* had taken to referring to Berlin as *Festung Berlin*, or "Hedgehog Berlin." When the newly appointed military commander of Berlin, Major General Hellmuth Reymann, took command on 6 March, he found little had been done to render Berlin defensible.

Of course, in a manner of speaking, Berlin was defensible, and had been so since 1941. That was when, in response to Allied bombing attacks, the first of six so-called Flak Towers had been erected. Berlin was not, and never really was, a fortress city. These towers represented the only form of defense it was believed Berlin required in the modern age, and why not? The city was last taken by foreign troops during the Seven Years' War.[61] At Humboldthain, Friedrichshain, and on the grounds of the Berlin Zoo, these leviathans were essentially antiaircraft forts, perfect expressions of Nazi tendencies toward gigantism and grandiosity. At the Zoo, at the southwest corner near the bird sanctuary, stood the most formidable of the Flak Towers. Two rooftop towers, L tower for communications, and G tower for main guns, dominated the structure, 132 feet high, covering a city block. Its walls of reinforced concrete were eight feet thick, and protecting its windows and firing embrasures were shutters of three- to four-inch-thick steel plates. Each corner of the tower was a gun tower in its own right, with multiple antiaircraft cannon. An ammunition elevator shuttled shells from a ground-floor magazine to the emplacements. Each tower served as an air raid shelter on the two lowest floors, a ninety-five-bed hospital, and warehouse. One of the floors at the Zoo Tower had been used to store art treasures from the Berlin museum, and another had been set aside for the headquarters of the *Deutschlandsender*, the national radio broadcasting system. The ordinary garrison was set at 100 men, but the Zoo Tower could hold 15,000 in an emergency. The garrison believed the Zoo Tower could hold out for a year, no matter what happened outside.[62]

Stalin did not give the Soviet Army a year to take Berlin. He gave it two weeks.[63] For this task, he authorized the use of three Soviet Fronts—the Second Belorussian, the First Belorussian, and the First Ukranian. The last two of these were commanded by marshals of the Soviet Union—Zhukov and Koniev—who were as much in competition with one another as with their duly authorized enemies. The three Fronts disposed more than 1.5 million men. Including other supports, the force dedicated to taking Berlin numbered 2.5 million men.[64]

The precise strength of German forces defending Berlin, either from behind the Oder-Niesse line or from behind the fringe of Berlin itself, cannot be determined, even today. Judging from later reports of military casualties or military prisoners, the number could have been as much as 500,000 in all, but between these numbers lay a great variance of soldierly skills, from the hardened veteran to the *Hitlerjugend* with their *panzerfausts*, or as the Russians called them, the *faustniki*.

Whenever military skills are at a premium, some physical additive is always called for, and here that meant field fortifications. By April, Soviet aerial reconnaissance photographs showed that Berlin had been encircled by three great defensive belts.[65] The first of these was sixty miles around and roughly followed the city edge. The second belt was much less broken than the first and integrated dominant buildings, railway cuttings, canals, bridges, and other urban terrain features, as well as the elevated railway system's lines. The final belt enclosed "the Citadel," which lay between the Spree River and the Landwehr Canal and was tied into the several Flak Towers. Inside the Citadel lay the *Reichstag*, the Ministry of the Interior, the *Reichskanzlei*, and Hitler's own bunker as well. From the center of the Citadel, designated sector "Z," eight other defense sectors radiated outward, each assigned a letter. The second ring was the place for soldiers to be if they had a choice; the Citadel was the place for the fanatical last stand.[66]

The Citadel was some seventy-five miles from the nearest Soviet forces and the point where they would begin to execute their plan. The Soviets' concept—written on the quick by Zhukov and Koniev over a twenty-four-hour period—was straightforward: beginning on 16 April, they would fight to encircle the city; penetrate it from the northeast, east, and southeast; and pass forward as many forces as possible to join with advancing Allied forces as they crossed the Elbe River to the west. This operation was not to be a leisurely siege: Stalin wanted it concluded by the end of the month.[67] And that, in effect, is what happened.

The main axis of the Soviet attack was to begin from Marshal Zhukov's bridgehead on the Oder River at Kustrin, which was due east and pointed directly at Berlin. As circumstances permitted, the two other Fronts, the Second Belorussian and the First Ukranian, would converge on the city from the northeast and south, respectively. On 16 April, Zhukov's artillery—with a density of 250 guns per kilometer—commenced the advance.[68]

In keeping with the slow collapse of national command and control inside Berlin, the forces meant to defend the city were unable to formulate any sort of unified plan of defense. The closer the Soviet offensive pressed on Berlin proper, the faster German formations disintegrated. Between the city and the Soviet advance lay the so-called "Army Group Vistula," nominally composed of the German Third and Ninth Armies, under the command of Colonel-General Gotthard Heinrici. One of the few professional soldiers left who were capable of commanding large formations, Heinrici hoped to keep the coming battle out of the city, but the weight of the Soviet offensive was too great. Heinrici's main task was to try to control the crash, but even that would prove too much. Within four days of the commencement of the offensive, the Soviets were on the fringes of the city. Within a week, nine Soviet armies were driving directly at the center of Berlin. The *Reichstag* was their aiming point, and on 30 April, two Soviet rifle divisions secured the above-ground part of the building only after fighting until midnight. Below ground, a much larger collection of Germans still would not surrender, some waiting until the last moment.[69] At 1500 on 2 May, Soviet forces officially ceased firing.

After two weeks of fighting, much of Berlin was demolished but not destroyed, and the distinction is important. None of the standard sources on the battle for Berlin detail precisely how much of the city suffered as a direct result of the battle. If one follows the trace of the Soviets' advance into the city, the western districts of Spandau, all the way down to Potsdam and perhaps even parts of Charlottenburg, seem to have escaped the maelstrom of battle that hit the city's center, "sector Z."

The human destruction can only be guessed at. As usual, noncombatants—that is, civilians unlikely to return fire—were at much greater risk than soldiers after the Dog Fight began. By one estimate, 100,000 civilians died, including 20,000 of heart attacks and 6,000 suicides. Almost all of the latter would have been women who meant either to preempt being raped or to punish themselves for having been raped. Where this particular crime was concerned, the conduct of the second and subsequent Soviet echelons added to the Red Army's already fearsome reputation, but it must be said that their much-criticized behavior was in keeping with ancient military traditions.[70]

The Soviets claim to have destroyed seventy infantry divisions, twelve Panzer divisions, and eleven motorized divisions, in the process taking some 480,000 prisoners. Within the city, Zhukov's and Koniev's armies took 134,000 prisoners. Operations against Berlin cost the Soviets 304,887 casualties from 16 April to 8 May. By the most conservative estimate, the battle for Berlin cost half a million casualties in all.[71]

The battle fought for Berlin was as close to total war as the world would come during the twentieth century. The war in Europe was not won in Berlin, nor lost there, nor indeed at any other single place. By 1945, cities alone no longer possessed the power to start and finish wars as they once did, and wars were no longer kept within strict geographical boundaries. During this birth of global war, other cities—many other cities—would suffer as much or more destruction, as many or more casualties, but being a victim of military attack is quite a different matter than being a battleground—and being a great symbolic battleground is even more different. At this remove, the battle for Berlin seems wholly gratuitous, pointless, but that is only the distortion of retrospect affecting our sight. The battle cannot be seen very clearly if one only analyzes costs and benefits. Seen from that perspective, the battle for Berlin evades reason altogether.

A Prussian from a different time would have understood Berlin as an example of what results when reason loses its grip over war. Carl von Clausewitz described "primordial violence, hatred and enmity" as one of three complex engines that by means of constant interaction move war.[72] By April 1945, all other considerations were subordinated to the impulse for revenge, creating a final campaign that was to be conducted without remorse. Stalin gave his two leading marshals little time to conceive how they might take Berlin, and some commentators have complimented how much they achieved in so short a time. But taking Berlin was hardly a great military puzzle. The most difficult part of the planning had more to do with accounting than with great strategy: it entailed the management of large bodies of armed force—bodies that were set for an ultimate convergence at the center of Berlin. There was no point in providing for contingencies because the *Wehrmacht* was in no condition to do much more than collect where they could and defend. Were it not for the assuaging of vengeance, Berlin might have been beside the point, too, but powerful motives of state were now directly entangling themselves in military operations. These had little to do with Berlin except as a symbol.

General Eisenhower's approach to the Berlin question was the reasonable one, of course. For him, Germany's power to resist still lay in the few viable military formations remaining. Once those formations were destroyed, Nazi Germany would be destroyed, regardless of what transpired in Berlin. Nothing in Berlin could change this proposition. This being so, as far as Eisenhower was concerned, there was no reason to carry the battlefield into the city. Of course, not everyone on Eisenhower's side felt the same way, Winston Churchill and Bernard Montgomery among them. The need for some sort of retribution naturally burned brighter in London than in Washington, but in Moscow it burned white-hot. None of the other Allies had such a claim on vengeance as the Russians, and when they broke into Berlin at the end of April, their uniforms stank with the joy of it.

What then, after all this time, does the battle of Berlin have to teach the modern military professional? As the inherent violence of war escalated in the twentieth century, the robustness of the city seemed to keep pace. If wars were more destructive, cities seemed capable of absorbing more destruction. No city was killed in the Second World War—neither Hamburg nor Dresden, Tokyo, Hiroshima, or Nagasaki. Since 1940, Berlin had been subjected to aerial attack, and yet five years later, only one-third of the city had been destroyed. In the remaining two-thirds, one assumes, city life continued with the requisite degree of cohesion. In early 1945, two and a half million people still lived in Berlin. Even if one assumes that *all* of the casualties from the battle of Berlin were taken from the resident population of the city, that would still leave two million souls, functioning more or less in concert with one another. Without that concert, Berlin would not have been possible. That the city continued to function reveals the strength of any great city's human and material superstructure—its cohesion as an urban entity. In the half-century since Berlin was last fought for, great cities of the world have been subjected to all manner of stresses. Not one has collapsed.

The place of the city in the world of war changed in the past two centuries. The power of decision in war lies elsewhere at the moment. The fortunes of a state no longer rise or fall on the fortunes of its cities. Cities play a part in modern war, but it is no longer a decisive part—at least, not for the moment. Is this perhaps about to change?

The Question of Asymmetry

Cities can be taken in two ways, from the outside or from the inside—that is, by invasion or by subversion. Of course, these are theoretical alternatives only. Reality is seldom so well organized. In actual practice, the invasion of a city has frequently been supported by friends inside the gates. The reverse is also true: urban subversives have sometimes made their plans contingent on an attack from outside at just the right moment.

Whether we characterize a certain conflict as invasive or subversive depends upon the nature of the aggressor. So, if the army outside bears the burden of the campaign, sets strategic purpose and direction, one can say that the conflict is invasive and that the subversive forces inside the city are essentially conducting an economy of force campaign. Think of the resistance inside Paris awaiting the arrival of Allied forces in 1944. On the other hand, if the subversives inside provide strategic purpose and direction, if in their absence the movement will collapse, the center of gravity is likely to be found inside the city cadre. In the first case, then, we have a "regular army to the rescue" scenario. In the second case, it is more the "someday my ship will come in" approach. Or the urban subversives may operate until they see a chance for a last dash to the finish line if they receive timely assistance from the outside. Those who fought their way along the Perfume River in Hue or through the Cholon District of a city that used to be called Saigon would need no reminder of how effective these combinations can be when they are properly executed.

Cities have always been attractive to subversive operations. They were good for these operations, just as they were good for other, less warlike reasons. The social, physical, and material density of cities lends greater effect to small actions. The killing of a policeman in a rural outstation, for instance, would produce a minor effect compared to a public assassination of that same policeman on the steps of Metropolitan police headquarters. Cities are conducive to an economy of effect. That is why they are attractive venues for unorthodox operations.

On 8 May 1945—Victory in Europe day—riots broke out during celebrations in the subprefecture of Setif in the French colony of Algeria. The violence lasted for one week, at the end of which several hundred *colons*—French settlers—were killed or injured. The official repression that followed lasted much longer and cost perhaps as many as ten times the number of Algerian lives as had been lost in the original uprising. The long-term result would not occur until almost thirty years later, when after an entire generation of revolutionary struggle, Algeria would regain its independence.

What happened in Setif had nothing whatever to do with the triumphs then being celebrated by the Great Powers. Nor did those who later came to lead the Algerian resistance, the *Partie Populaire Algerienne* (PPA), have the slightest compunction about departing from the hoary military canons of the western world—if, indeed, they were much aware of them. Over the last half century the PPA, and parties around the world of many shapes and stripes, set themselves in opposition to established order and availed themselves of any possible advantage over their enemies. In the process, these unorthodox forces have directly challenged the monopoly of military power formerly enjoyed by professional armies, sometimes to the ultimate discomfort of the professionals. Indeed, Algeria's modern history is a perfect case in point.[73]

After centuries of military history in which combat strength correlated with physical mass, professional armies are fearful that, under certain conditions, a large, highly evolved military system may be a handicap. This paradox, which has never been entirely absent from the world of war, has been given impetus by the technological progress of the last half century.[74] Truly dramatic technical achievements and their rapid diffusion around the world place power within the reach of unorthodox forces that they would not otherwise enjoy. An imagined clash between these newly empowered unorthodox forces and the forces of orthodoxy has excited no small amount of literature in professional military journals. One result has been to give rise to the notion of "asymmetry."

The career of "asymmetry" as a modern military concept is indicative of the theoretical void in which orthodox twenty-first-century military forces will be attempting to operate. In the absence of any practical theoretical foundation or any authoritative or organizing principles, military professionals are left defenseless against slogans, which, if they are not really useful, nonetheless comfort the ignorant. "Asymmetry" is a good example of what happens when an incompletely thought-out notion degenerates rapidly to slogan. Briefly, "asymmetry" is defined by those who have an equal contempt for language and fact as the relationship between widely dissimilar military forces in conflict with one another. This asymmetry, whatever its source, conveys upon its beneficiary an overwhelming advantage in the war, conflict, operation, or contest.[75]

Insofar as "asymmetry" is and always has been an ineluctable element of war, one would think it so obvious as to deserve little further comment. It would be a strange army indeed that did not seek an advantage of some kind over its enemy. In war, the idea of a "fair" or "equitable" fight is fantastic. And to suggest that seeking an advantage is in any way unusual or unworthy is evidence of a certain lack of knowledge about war itself. That asymmetric warfare would be associated with urban warfare is significant.

Cities have always been important because we have made them so, and we have always been of at least two minds about what we have made. Cities excite our pride, but they also excite our fear. Cities are seen as the embodiment of our civilization, but they are also places where humankind can act in the most uncivilized ways. For Fernand Braudel, cities were like "electric transformers . . . they increase tension, accelerate the rhythm of exchange and constantly recharge human life. . . ." Cities are all these things and more. "World history is city history," wrote Oswald Spengler in his classic, *The Decline of the West*. Max Weber, another well-known student of the city, was hardly in Spengler's class as a pessimist, but on this they agreed: cities reflected the state of civilization that sustained them.[76]

World megacities—urban agglomerations, as demographers have taken to calling them—now express the state of globalized civilization. Now, the world has more cities than ever, and more important cities than ever. The great cities of the past are greater still, and all demographic projections agree that these will keep pace with patterns of growth and distribution. Commentators and analysts who have found cause only for despair would be interested to learn that these projections are well within the compass of historical experience and that civilization did not implode under their weight. As Braudel explained some time ago, "all major bursts of growth are expressed by an urban explosion."[77]

It is no good arguing that cities are intrinsically unstable social systems. For every unstable city, however defined, thousands more work with machine-like effectiveness. Projecting our anxieties onto the broad screen of urban globalism merely obscures the important by emphasizing the uncomfortable. However, one aspect of modern urban development that directly influences the military art has in fact attained a state of development that warrants further discussion here.

The Invisible City

Late in the twentieth century, a new kind of city was created, invisible but by no means imaginary. This is the city built by the information revolution, and it is leading to the transformation of global life. The great cities of the world are merely the first to see the consequences of this transformation, the first to experience its most far-reaching effect. For our purposes, it is enough at the moment to recognize the phenomenon and allow it a place in this discussion.

The first and most likely practical effect of this transformation will be felt on how military problems are perceived. We have no difficulty imagining how much physical space a given city occupies. When we learn that in 1945 Berlin's circumference was sixty-five miles, our imagination can at least make a start at estimating the kind, size, and shape of force that might be able to take the city at that time. Our understanding of modern cities, however, is a good deal less confident. When we consider the challenges posed by dozens of skyscrapers collected in one dense district, underground public transport systems, and suburbs reaching for mile upon irregular mile, we are on thinner ice.

And now, the professional imagination will have to contend with an even more complex challenge—indeed, more complex by several orders of magnitude. We need only contemplate the epitome of the modern megacity, Hong Kong, to appreciate just how complex that challenge can be. A great number of the world's more congested cities might well hold Hong Kong in admiration for its ability to deal with both congestion and prosperity, for the great part of Hong Kong's recent growth has not been expressed physically so much as cybernetically. Today, 85.2 percent of Hong Kong's entire economy is configured in this way. At the moment, Hong Kong's is the most highly concentrated service-sector economy in the world.[78] But much of what occurs in Hong Kong occurs *only* in cyberspace—the invisible reflection of the city itself. The "space" not only occupied but also the space influenced by this invisible city is critical to the entire East Asian regional economy and no small part of the global economy as well. Furthermore, the correlation between evident physical prosperity and virtual prosperity is a good deal more tenuous. One would be mistaken, for instance, to draw inferences between the physical appearance of the major cities of India and their cybernetic identities: the Indian subcontinent is now regarded as "one of the world's powerhouses" in computer software programming.[79]

Any city may be seen as expressing itself in this way, which could be described as its "cybernetic signature." Two centuries ago, the number of ships anchored in the lower Thames reflected London's role in global capital expansion. Similar indicators can be seen today in the real-time reports on the World Wide Web of the "Interweather," the status of global data flow.[80] For our purposes, the birth of this new kind of city means that its place in global cyberspace—its cybernetic signature—must be included as an essential element in strategic, operational, and perhaps even tactical planning in some instances.

Now the question becomes one of the role this new city will play in future warfare, a question that is fervently discussed but still far from being answered. How do these developments in global urbanism affect military operations as the United States might conduct them in the opening decades of the twenty-first century? What are the implications for the military art, science, and above all, practice?

Notes

1. Said to have been conducted between 585 and 573 B.C.

2. Paul Bentley Kern, *Ancient Siege Warfare* (London: Souvenir Press, 1999), 69.

3. Tercius Chandler and Gerald Fox, *3000 Years of Urban Growth* (London: Academic Press, 1974), 80-82, 219, 223, 232-35, 247, 265.

4. Quoted in Kern, *Ancient Siege Warfare*, 68.

5. Sun Tzu, *The Art of War*, trans. with an introduction by Samuel B. Griffith, with a foreword by B. H. Liddell Hart (Oxford: Oxford University Press, 1963), 79.

6. Thucydides, *History of the Peloponnesian War*, trans. by Rex Warner (London: Penguin Books, 1988), 125-26.

7. Kern, *Ancient Siege Warfare*, 97, 103.

8. Ibid., 103-4. That is, all will be killed or sold into slavery.

9. Tacitus, *The Complete Works of Tacitus*, trans. by Alfred John Church and William Jackson Bodribb, eds., with an introduction by Moses Hadas (New York: The Modern Library, 1942), 543-58. R. Ernest Dupuy and Trevor N. Dupuy, *Encyclopedia of Military History from 3500 B.C. to the Present* (New York: Harper & Row, 1970), 127-28.

10. Mumford, *City in History*, 209.

11. Tacitus, *The Complete Works*, 549.

12. Ibid., 549.

13. In which cases, being unsalable, the slaves were killed if their families would not pay ransom.

14. Tacitus, *The Complete Works*, 550-58.

15. Dupuy and Dupuy, *Encyclopedia of Military History*, 619. N.a., "Cremona," *Microsoft Encarta Encyclopedia 99*, p. 1, CD-ROM.

16. Geoffrey Parker, *The Army of Flanders and the Spanish Road, 1567-1659* (Cambridge: Cambridge University Press, 1972), 10.

17. J. W. Wijn, "Military Forces and Warfare," in *The New Cambridge Modern History*, vol. 4, ed. by J. P. Cooper (Cambridge: Cambridge University Press, 1970), 222-23; see also Parker, *The Army of Flanders*, 8-10.

18. Kostof, *The City Shaped*, 69.

19. David P. Jordan, *Transforming Paris: The Life and Labors of Baron Haussmann* (Chicago: University of Chicago Press, 1995), 18-23.

20. Ibid., 188.

21. The first Viking raid of 845 A.D. was followed in 885 by a full-fledged, eleven-month-long siege. The third, by Otto, emperor of the Holy Roman Empire, was lifted only when an epidemic broke out in the lines. Those of 1418, 1436, 1570, and 1649 arose from internal struggles for power and civil wars, while that of 1814 would lead to Napoleon's abdication and exile. The siege of 1944 was technically a "liberation" in that the city had been occupied by the German army since 1940. Dupuy and Dupuy, *Encyclopedia of Military History*, 246-52, 258, 415-17, 481, 560, 763, and 1108.

22. Michael Howard, *The Franco-Prussian War* (London: Methuen, 1961), 229, 317-19, 371.

23. The crown prince, writing in his personal war diary, is quoted in Howard, *The Franco-Prussian War*, 351, 353.

24. Howard, *The Franco-Prussian War*, 352.

25. Ibid., 250.

26. Gunther E. Rothenberg, "Moltke, Schlieffen, and the Doctrine of Strategic Envelopment," in *Makers of Modern Strategy: From*

Machiavelli to the Nuclear Age, ed. by Peter Paret (Princeton, NJ: Princeton University Press, 1986), 306-7; see also Howard, *The Franco-Prussian War*, 455.

27. Michael Howard, *The Franco-Prussian War*, 326.

28. Giulio Douhet's *Command of the Air*, as the bible of air power enthusiasts, still states the case more clearly than any of his successors. His views and those of other like-minded theorists are conveniently summarized in Gerhard Weinberg, *A World at Arms: A Global History of World War II* (Cambridge: Cambridge University Press, 1994), 574-76.

29. Ibid., 149-50.

30. See two different interpretations of the objective of the raid on Guernica in Hugh Thomas, *The Spanish Civil War* (New York: Harper Colophon Books, 1961), 419-23; and Peter Wyden, *The Passionate War: The Narrative History of the Spanish Civil War* (New York: Simon and Schuster, 1983), 349-63.

31. Robert Goralski, *World War II Almanac: A Political and Military Record* (New York: G. P. Putnam's Sons, 1981), 130-33.

32. J. Bowyer Bell, *Besieged: Seven Cities Under Siege* (New York: Chilton Publishers, 1966), 56-57.

33. Ibid., 57, 61.

34. Ibid., 61, 67.

35. Goralski, *World War II Almanac*, 395.

36. See the portrait of Tokyo immediately after surrender drawn in John Dower's *Embracing Defeat: Japan in the Wake of World War II* (New York: W. W. Norton, 1999), 44-48.

37. A photo of what remains of Lidice today can be found in Kostof, *The City Assembled*, 257.

38. Fernand Braudel, *The Identity of France*, vol.1, *History and Environment*, trans. by Sian Reynolds (New York: Harper & Row, 1990), 312-15, 330-35.

39. General von Falkenhayn is quoted in Michael Geyer, "German Strategy in the Age of Machine Warfare, 1914-1945," in Paret, *Makers of Modern Strategy*, 534. See also Eugen Weber, *A Modern History of Europe: Men, Cultures, and Societies from the Renaissance to the Present* (New York: W. W. Norton & Co., 1971), 774-76.

40. Michael Geyer, "German Strategy in the Age of Machine Warfare," 535.

41. Ibid., 535.

42. Ibid., 536.

43. Weinberg, *A World at Arms*, 411.

44. Ibid., 42.

45. John Erickson, *The Road to Stalingrad: Stalin's War against Germany*, vol. 1 (New York: Harper and Row, 1975), 362-64.

46. Ibid., 384.

47. Ibid., 387.

48. Antony Beevor, *Stalingrad: The Fateful Siege: 1942-1943* (New York: Viking Press, 1998), 161.

49. Beevor, *Stalingrad*, 123-24, 128-29, 147. Weinberg, *A World at Arms*, 447-53.

50. Erickson, *The Road to Stalingrad*, 387. After their successful assault carried German troops all the way to the river on 13 September, several boats of considerable size carrying civilian refugees were taken under fire. One thousand refugees died when a larger steamer was sunk. Clearly, no small number of civilians were in the city and still trying to escape, with or without state permission.

51. Erickson, *Road to Stalingrad*, 421.

52. Beevor, *Stalingrad*, 439.

53. Ibid., 148.

54. Ibid., 190-93.

55. Erickson, *The Road to Stalingrad*, 431.

56. Stalin's cable is reproduced in all the standard sources. See, for instance, Erickson, *The Road to Stalingrad*, 528-29.

57. See Cornelius Ryan, *The Last Battle* (New York: Simon and Schuster, 1966), 321. The phrase and the estimate are both Omar Bradley's. Some Americans, professional soldiers, were disappointed not to be going to Berlin for that reason. See the exchange between General Simpson and one of his brigadier generals in Erickson, *Road to Stalingrad*, 552.

58. Ryan, *The Last Battle*, 399.

59. Ibid., 27.

60. Ibid., 380.

61. Berlin was periodically occupied during the Napoleonic Wars, but after the Austrians took the city in 1760, it had not been the object of a campaign or the site of a battle.

62. Ryan, *The Last Battle,* 166-67. At the height of the battle, 30,000 people were said to have taken refuge here.

63. Weinberg, *A World at Arms*, 822.

64. Ryan, *The Last Battle,* 256. Weinberg, *A World at Arms*, 822. The first writer cites figures from forces immediately engaged, while the second obviously includes rear supports as well.

65. Erickson, *The Road to Berlin,* 535.

66. Ryan, *The Last Battle*, 381.

67. Weinberg, *A World at Arms,* 821-22, conveniently summarizes the Soviet plan and the circumstances of its composition. A more detailed account can be found in Erickson, *The Road to Berlin,* 531-39.

68. By now, this was the standard artillery density for launching an operation of this magnitude. As Soviet forces closed in on the

city, the densities would increase. At Teltow canal, they would reach 650 per kilometer. See Erickson, *The Road to Berlin*, 586-87.

69. Ibid., 590, 604.

70. Ryan, *The Last Battle*, 520.

71. See Erickson, *The Road the Berlin*, 595; and Ryan, *The Last Battle*, 520.

72. Carl von Clausewitz, *On War*, ed. and trans. by Michael Howard and Peter Paret (New York: Everyman's Library, 1993), 101. The military savant will recognize this passage as one of the elements of Clausewitz's celebrated "trinity of war."

73. Alistair Horne, *A Savage War of Peace: Algeria, 1954-1962* (New York: Penguin Books, 1977), 23-28, and *passim*.

74. Walter Millis, *Arms and Men: A Study of American Military History* (New York: The New American Library, 1956), 272-307, addresses this paradox in his discussion of nuclear weapons policy and its effect on traditional military action.

75. See, for instance, Lloyd Matthews, ed., *Challenging the United States Symmetrically and Asymmetrically: Can America be Defeated?* (Carlisle Barracks, PA: US Army War College, 1998), particularly, Charles Dunlap, Jr., "Preliminary Observations: Asymmetrical Warfare and the Western Mindset." One of the most interesting entries in the growing asymmetry literature comes to the West from two officers in China's People's Liberation Army, Colonels Qiao Liang and Wang Xiangsui, in a book entitled *Unrestricted Warfare*, published in February 1999, by Beijing's PLA Literature and Arts Publishing House, suggesting a semi-official approval. Only part of this study has been translated into English by the CIA. The authors turn asymmetry into a grand strategy, since it seems hopeless to them that China or any other country can keep technical and economic pace with the United States. Copy in author's possession.

76. Max Weber, *The City*, trans. and ed. by Don Martindale and Gertrud Neuwirth (Glencoe, IL: The Free Press, 1958), 36. Weber approvingly quotes Spengler's *Decline of the West* here.

77. Fernand Braudel, *The Structures of Everyday Life*, vol. 1, *Civilization and Capitalism, 15th-18th Century*, trans. by Sian Reynolds (New York: Harper and Row, 1981), 479-81

78. Hong Kong Trade Development Council, "Hong Kong & China Economies," 11 January 2000, 5, at <www.tdc.org.hk/main/economic.htm>.

79. John Zubrizycki, "Mastering Software Helps India Youths Snag Foreign Jobs," *Christian Science Monitor OnLine*, 13 November 1997, received via Internet, 29 February 2000.

80. See "Checking the Interweather," *Time Digital Daily, 20 December 1999*, at <www.pathfinder.com/time/digital/daily>.

Copyright 1999/Haruki Murakami
Reprinted by Permission of International Creative Management, Inc.

Part of the route map Tokyo's public transit system. One need not be a master of Japanese to see the choke point at Shinjuku Station.

Part Three

Metropolis, or Modern Urban Warfare

The Global Metropolis and Strategic Anxiety

Nearly thirty years ago, it was estimated that a modern army, employing current US Army organization, training, doctrine, tactics, and materiel, would require seven years to "clear" Los Angeles.[1]

Tokyo: 28.8 million. Mexico City: 17.8 million. Sao Paolo: 17.5 million. New York: 16.5 million. Have megacities outgrown the military art? Have these urban agglomerations grown so large and so complex that they cannot by any means be traversed, subdued, occupied, or conquered?

- Is the military art up to this?

- At this moment, the answer must be no.

Urban warfare does not have its Clausewitz, nor is it ever likely to. Neither centuries of experience nor libraries groaning under the weight of case studies have been sufficient to create a reliable and practical theory of war as it is conducted in the urban environment. Professionals and amateurs alike have been forced to try it out on the ground.

But trying it out on the ground is not the best answer. It is not even a good answer. One becomes a victim of surprise. Old mistakes are repeated. Effort better spent elsewhere is wasted. The higher costs of fighting in this environment are made costlier. Time becomes even less friendly than it was. One could lose before getting it right. One has less time to win these days. One feels the weight of limitations upon the employment of national force, even as some forecasts point toward a conflict-ridden world.

The fusion of urban growth and global growth has given rise to no small degree of semiofficial hand wringing and crisis mongering. The prospect of an urbanized world excites reactionary impulses in otherwise sober minds. Only bad things can come from such a future: unwholesome congestion, crime and decadence, disease, civil strife, subversion, and even war. Global urbanization is assumed to engender conflict, some of which must inevitably blossom into real war. Of course, most of the real trouble, it is assumed, will be in the Third World.[2] Trends culminate there.

- Most of these assumptions are wrong, or wrongheaded.
- War is *not* on the rise—neither between nor within states.

Ethnic conflicts are *not* more numerous. Conflicts often depicted as "ethnic" are actually struggles between different *cultures,* not *ethnic groups*. An accounting by *The New York Times* in 1993, which has been widely cited, appears on closer inspection to have misrepresented the ethnic nature of half of the forty-eight conflicts it recorded as being under way at the time. In fact, the term "ethnic" is now so widely misused as to have lost all meaning. When wars occur today, it appears they occur for the same reasons they have always occurred: power or territory.[3]

Acts of terrorism are *not* increasing in frequency. Terrorist attacks are at their lowest worldwide levels since the 1960s, when modern terrorism was inaugurated by the Black September movement. In March 1995, Japan's radical *Aum Shinrikyo* cult achieved instant world recognition when it killed twelve people and injured 6,000 by releasing Sarin gas in several of Tokyo's public transit stations.[4] For several days, authorities were forced to close *parts* of the city's transport system, but Tokyo could not close and did not have to close. The bombings of the World Trade Center in New York and the Murrah Building in Oklahoma City etched themselves in the national psychology, but in neither case was any lasting goal achieved. In these three instances, there is the common thread of unproductive violence: all are, paradoxically, antiwar, in that the goal was not to win but to punish. In any case, global urbanization cannot be considered as a contributing factor to these actions.

The strategic misapprehensions do not limit themselves to the general public, to the officially innocent. That is why it is necessary to return to fundamentals for the moment, in which our first task is to distinguish between that which is true of American strategy in general and that which is true of American strategy when there is a prospect of urban operations. As we have seen, even the shadow of an urban presence seems to distort perceptions that in other cases would be quite straightforward. Therefore, we should begin by briefly describing the shape of American strategy, at this point, as a series of propositions:

In the aftermath of the Cold War, the United States is the most powerful nation in the world.

- The United States is thus the first among Great Powers.

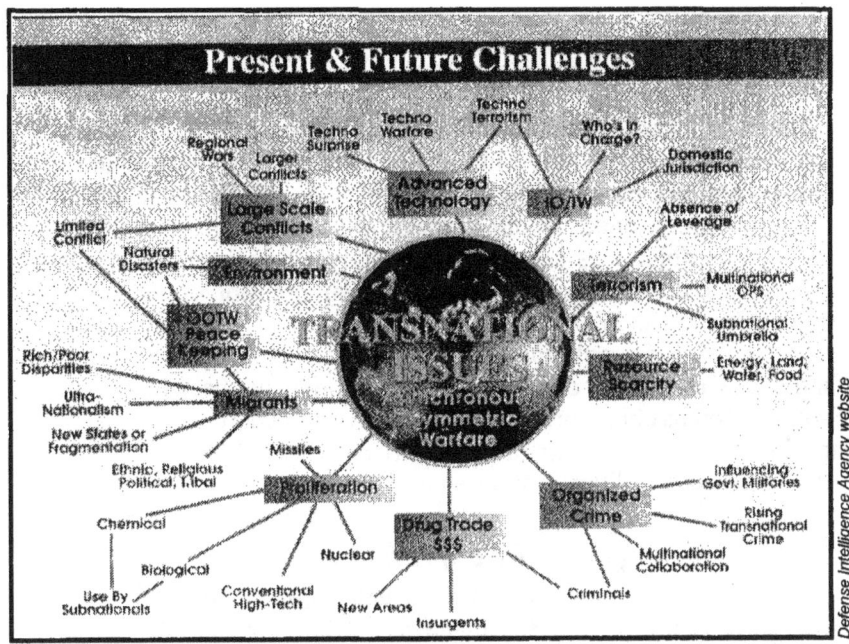

The Laundry list

- The United States' strategy is thus a global strategy.
- The United States generally exercises its strategic power by non-military means.
- The United States has not renounced the use of aggressive force.
- The United States prefers to employ its armed forces in reaction to armed aggression.
- Having conducted a strategic retrenchment, the continental United States now exercises strategic command and control and is now the strategic base of deployment for all American military operations.
- This strategic retrenchment has given subsequent American military operations an expeditionary character.
- The expeditionary character of American military operations is in consonance with longstanding national preferences that require

limitations in terms of purpose, time, geographical extent, size of deployment, and force permitted.

Taken as a whole, these propositions aim at limiting the exercise of American military power. Indeed, a certain continuity with the fundamental principles of Cold War strategy can be detected here. Gradually conditioned by our strategic policies during the past half century, the objectives toward which today's principles are directed have more to do with the containment and suppression of war than the prosecution of it. We are not so very far, after all, from Bernard Brodie's classic formulation of deterrence, first coined in 1945: "Thus far the chief purpose of our military establishment has been to win wars. From now on its chief purpose must be to avert them. It can have almost no other purpose."[5] Within the boundaries of Brodie's "almost," nearly all of American military history since 1945 has been made.

American Strategy and the Expeditionary Option

The most intense politico-military rivalry of the Cold War occurred during its first thirty years, from 1946 to 1976. These were the "years of maximum danger," when all parties were learning how to function in a new world dominated by nuclear superpowers, and when every military action—threatened or real—contained the germ of a fatal escalation toward general war.

It was during this period that the armed forces of the United States, in particular, showed a certain talent for modern expeditionary operations. Indeed, the record is unparalleled. Between 1946 and 1976, the armed forces of the United States conducted 215 expeditionary operations. Put differently, the United States employed a significant part of its armed forces for expeditionary purposes, on average, once every other month for thirty years.[6]

Usually, these deployments lasted about ninety days. Most were relatively minor operations; that is, their objectives were limited. The troop strength of these expeditions was likewise limited. The Army was involved in thirty-nine of these expeditionary operations, commonly at a strength of at least multiple battalions, and up to more than a division on several occasions. Reserve forces were mobilized on only three occasions.[7]

In the days before plentiful airlift and sealift, proximity to the operational area was of primary importance. This, in keeping with tradition, made naval forces the expeditionary forces of choice. In nearly two-thirds of these expeditions, American naval forces were already close at hand, and the expedition employed whatever force was present. More than half of all the expeditions involving ground forces were conducted by the Marines. Expeditions that lasted longer sometimes excited a supplementary deployment of Army troops, as in the case of the Lebanon intervention of 1958, when more than a division was eventually sent to the area, as well as a sizeable Air Force contingent.

A goodly part of these expeditions fell into the general category of "showing the force," for which aircraft carriers were most often employed. Sixty percent of all these contingency operations were primarily conducted by the Navy, and the majority of those involved a carrier presence. But the presence of a carrier offshore, while a well-known and understood means of signaling American interest, did not affect the outcome of the operation so much as direct, on-the-ground presence by Marines or Army troops. Direct force, in other words, worked a more positive result in a shorter time than indirect force or posturing.[8]

Expeditionary operations have been the form of choice for the United States for the better part of the twentieth century, and it is easy enough to see why. An expedition promises no "foreign entanglements" because it does not usually entail a commitment beyond its immediate purpose. Ordinarily, the expected end-state is unambiguous, a problem with a solution. An expedition is not ordinarily meant to work vast changes in a local situation, although modern history is replete with examples in which foreign armies have descended upon hapless regimes in order to effect a change in rulers.

As a type of operation, the expedition takes on the air of an emergency, an unexpected mission in which certain operational preferences or material preferences are sometimes sacrificed for the sake of speed. Emergencies ordinarily demand a quick response, but whether quick or not, it is the *effective* response that is wanted in the end. Quick responses may be less desirable than effective responses, as American policymakers decided after the Iraqi invasion of Kuwait.[9] Perhaps because of this perception of a speedy operation, we commonly think of expeditions as tending toward the smaller size, but as we have seen, there is no intrinsic reason for this to be so. Expeditions can be very large, indeed, and they can also be very slow, as the American expeditionary forces in both world wars, as well as the expedition to the Persian Gulf in 1990 demonstrated. But these examples may stretch the point to breaking. The common variety of

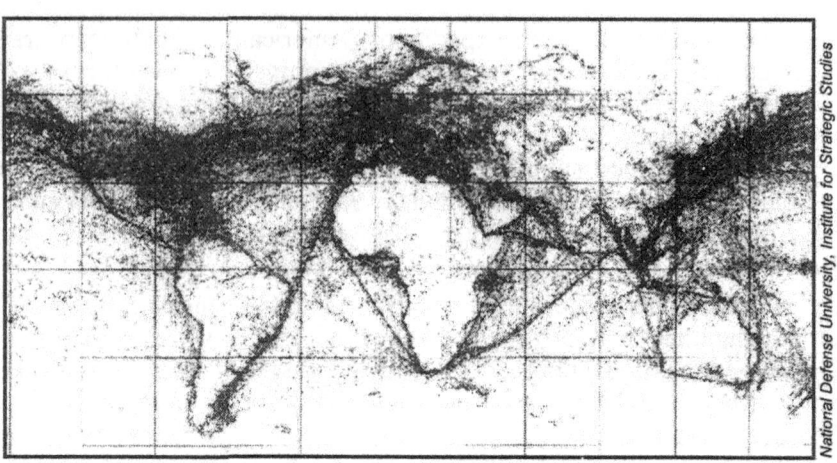
An electromagnetic spectrum satellite photo of global
lines of communication, 1999

expedition begins modestly and, one hopes, concludes in the same way. Ideally, the intervening party expects to enjoy the initiative throughout the course of its operation and may be retractable or expansible, as policy and circumstances dictate—for the expedition always begins its life as a strategic operation.

In the past, the expedition seems to have lent itself much more readily to direct political control than more complex or extended operations, but this advantage may be gradually disappearing in the face of quantum improvements in command and control technology. Today, the size or complexity of an operation is much less likely to shield commanders from strategic direction. Even during the Gulf War, allied forces appear to have had technical command and control capacity to spare. More than sixty Western military satellites were pressed into service along with several more commercial satellites. When the operation was in full swing, forces in theater placed 700,000 calls and 152,000 messages a day. Communications systems managed some 30,000 radio frequencies for constant service. According to one study, in at least one case, the capacity of these systems far outpaced their content: 80 percent of all intelligence traffic was reported as "redundant."[10] The implications of these technical developments are even now poorly appreciated.

Since time immemorial, soldiers have complained of "interference" from on high, of not having been given sufficient latitude to direct operations.[11] They will have much cause for complaint in the future. All the trends in modern command and control systems conduce to more, not less, control at all echelons of action—so much so that one might well pose a new rule for soldiering in the cybernetic age: *Whatever can be controlled, will be controlled.* Strategic direction will be more intrusive—a term which implies only occasional, if annoying, interruption—but more insistent, too, more *commanding*, gradually assuming decisions once monopolized by commanders on the spot, happy that their masters were great distances away. No more.

There is one other characteristic of the expeditionary record that is operationally significant: in almost half—104 of the 215 expeditions recorded—an urban area was an intrinsic element of the operation.[12] Expeditionary operations stand an increasingly good chance of occurring in an urban area as time goes on. Expeditionary operations and urban operations, therefore, form a nexus—a crossroads of the modern military art.

Certain aspects of these operational patterns have changed since the conclusion of the Cold War. Late in 1995, the Army announced that its deployment tempos had increased by 300 percent, the result, first, of new conflicts no longer being suppressed by the Cold War, and second, of the concomitant retrenchment of strategic deployments and reductions in end strength. Although a highly dubious statistic, to say the least, it does point to an important new development in the international climate.[13] Cold War interventions were more likely to be unilateral than today, when American armed forces find themselves as part of larger multinational formations, often operating under the authority of the United Nations. Earlier, with the threat of a Soviet veto hanging over any Cold War undertaking Washington might have proposed for the UN's consideration, the United States had little choice but to act singly. And, after all, many of the American expeditions in those days were conducted as yet another move in the great bipolar superpower game.

Since the Cold War, a more compliant Russian stance in the UN Security Council has benefited the United States and the western European nations, who have found that there are certain political and operational advantages to be gained from operating under UN auspices. In what one scholar has called "the intervention dilemma," western public opinion in recent years, while disapproving in general of military intervention, also insists increasingly that "something be done" to alleviate crises. As a result, crisis intervention in the service of peacekeeping or "good offices" missions increased from ten operations a year in the 1980s to twenty operations a year in the first half of the 1990s.[14]

At the same time, a much more active United Nations contributed to a significant increase in the frequency of expeditions. Cold War barriers to unanimity in the Security Council having been resolved for the most part (although China does continue to use its veto power), the leading western nations are not only able to intervene more easily, they are willing to intervene as well. One reason is that the scruples against interfering in the internal affairs of sovereign nations, and the adherence to the right of national self-determination, are challenged by a new trend to establish and enforce certain minimal international standards of performance for member states, especially where individual human rights are thought to be in jeopardy. Interventions in the internal affairs of "failed states" have increased dramatically from five operations per year in the 1980s to seventeen per year during the 1990s.[15] It was under precisely these circumstances that the Americans found themselves leading the Unified Task Force, or UNITAF, into Somalia late in 1992.[16] One must assume, under the circumstances, that such "international taskings" as these will increase in frequency.

So much for the strategic context in which the United States now finds itself. Although the framework in which our armed forces operate today is far different from that of only a decade ago, strategic principles have not changed so much as strategic policy. Clausewitz would say that, although the ends have changed, the ways and means are not substantially different from before. The military operations launched by the United States in aid of its international objectives seem not to have changed their general form so much, falling routinely into the category of expeditionary operations broadly defined. Even Operation Desert Storm could be categorized in this way, allowing for its greater magnitude. So while the expedition is one of the most time-honored forms of military operation one could imagine, it has proved itself an infinitely flexible form of operation. At the moment, the expedition is the form of military operation that best suits the strategic canvas on which we must act for the foreseeable future. Just as earlier times have been noted for their adherence to one form of war or another, or even one operational style, it may well be that the turn of this century will be seen as a period typified by expeditionary operations. That is the premise on which we shall now proceed.

Tradition and Progress in the Military Art

In old military textbooks and field manuals, strategic purpose and direction manifest themselves at the tactical level of war. Tactics produce what strategy demands. Quite often, one finds the supposition that a tactical success might compensate for strategic miscalculation so that no matter how far astray policy may wander, true tactical skill is what counts in the end. It is quite amazing how many modern soldiers still subscribe to this ancient vision of warfighting.

In practice, the relationships between the different levels of war bear little resemblance to textbook descriptions of whatever vintage. Perhaps these relationships are best described in more modern language as *interactive*. All the same, it is still possible for professional soldiers to superimpose upon war a kind of fictitious order as a means of dealing with these interactions. As in days of old, this approach assumes that military techniques, if properly and constantly drilled, can overcome any problem posed by process, by the enemy, or by the environment in which the fighting is to be done. For lack of a better term, we can call this the *instrumental* approach, and it is a habit that a materially rich army acquires over time. Others have called this conception of war materialistic, "force-on-force," or "attrition-oriented," but neither of these terms quite conveys the idea—*as it acts*. For Edward Luttwak in the early 1980s, such conceptions were hopelessly crude and wasteful:

> In the extreme case of pure attrition, there are only techniques and tactics, and there is no action at all at the operational level. All that remains are routinized techniques of reconnaissance, movement, resupply, etc. to bring firepower-producing forces within range of the most conveniently targetable aggregations of enemy forces and supporting structures. Each set of targets is then to be destroyed by the cumulative effect of firepower, victory being achieved when the proportion destroyed suffices to induce retreat or surrender, or theoretically, when the full inventory of enemy forces is destroyed.[17]

At the tactical level, we can recognize this conception in action when the Red Army cleared snipers during the Battle of Berlin by means of artillery, essentially the same techniques that survive today in the first and second battles of Grozny. But we can see in Luttwak's passage a prescient description of how the Americans fought the war in the Gulf at the operational level as well.[18] In essence, weight—by numbers and volume of fire—substitutes for technique. Naturally, this conception of war assigns less value to operational velocity and precise execution. Older, industrial-style armies do not have the tools necessary to execute modern warfare—and that includes intellectual tools as well. Older-style armies are attuned well enough to fight in the open field environment, where instrumentalism finds its best expression. Some armies have no choice but to operate in this way. Some armies are struggling to break free of instrumental warfare, and some are merely struggling to preserve tradition.

For nearly two decades, the US Army has subscribed, officially at least, to the style of military thought called the operational art. In the arcane world of military theory, the operational art roughly takes the place once occupied by grand tactics. The primary function of grand tactics was simply to make possible what strategy imagined. Grand tactics, as a level of war, was defined in various ways during its heyday in the eighteenth and nineteenth centuries—for instance by geography or terrain or by relationship to enemy formations—but the fundamental use for grand tactics was that it put forces in place, at the ready, for the tactician to employ when the time came to engage the enemy. But under grand tactics, the tactical act was still an event, not a process—a sip of the wine, but not the bottle.

Grand tactics, long since lapsed into obscurity, was supplanted by the imposition of the operational art as it was conceived in the US Army in the early 1980s. But because the operational art was the principal means by which the US Army's new "AirLand Battle" doctrine of the early 1980s was explained, it has often been confused as doctrine itself. This is how the AirLand Battle was rendered officially in its fullest expression in the 1986 edition of FM 100-5:

> The object of all operations is to impose our will upon the enemy.... To do this we must throw the enemy off balance with a powerful blow from an unexpected direction, follow-up rapidly to prevent his recovery and continue operations aggressively to achieve the higher commander's goals. The best results are obtained when powerful blows are struck against critical units or areas whose loss will degrade the coherence of enemy operations in depth.[19]

As one close student of Army doctrine has observed, "AirLand Battle is an application of classic twentieth-century maneuver theory for mechanized forces."[20] The doctrine presupposed an enemy rich in numbers and material weight, organized, trained, and equipped much like oneself, but with enough of a difference to permit a qualitative edge—such as, for instance, superior training—to become the key to victory. The flow of battle imagined by the doctrine was nearly continuous. The enemy's superstructure found its strength from its echelonment to a great depth, but happily, that was where the enemy's center of gravity could be found too. But the AirLand Battle was not conceived as an attritional doctrine; finesse was critical to one's success, in fact. One had to deal the winning blow on the enemy's center of gravity by an indirect route or means.

Of course, the doctrine was specifically tailored for fighting the Soviets in NATO Europe, but it managed to travel to the Gulf War, where conditions for its application seemed appropriate. Notwithstanding its presumed success in the desert, AirLand Battle is not quite the doctrine for all seasons, nor was it ever intended to be.[21] The operational art is another matter entirely, however. As a mode of systematic military analysis, the operational art seemed equal to the demands made of it, regardless of the mission or location.

Just as with any set of complex ideas actually applied over a period of time, the operational art has been domesticated during the past two decades, worn down to a shape that practitioners could accept. Along the way, a collection of conceptual tools has evolved to assist in its application.[22] Some of these have been lifted directly from classical military theory, others from less exalted heights. All are now as deeply embedded in the Army's warfighting psyche as any in memory.

The planning and execution of the theater-level campaign was the focus of the operational art when it was conceived. The campaign plan itself was the mechanism by which strategic direction was to be translated into a highly coordinated sequence of interrelated tactical actions that would move one's war toward the attainment of strategic objectives. Second in importance only to defining one's mission was defining the enemy's "center of gravity," a notion which derived from the Clausewitzian idea that, within any enemy body, a point could be found that served as the source of all power. The center of gravity is the *sine qua non* of an enemy's capacity to resist the imposition of one's own will upon him. However, sometimes the center of gravity proved to be rather elusive, not quite as straightforwardly identifiable as one might hope. So concessions to practicality were made that permitted the modern operational artist to identify several "centers of gravity," thus making nonsense of the original idea, but verging along the way with another of these planner's tools—the concept of the "decisive point" and its subset, "objective points."

Under the terms of this concept, the seizure of decisive points permits one's forces to advance toward the center (or centers) of gravity by means of the battles and engagements already determined upon and planned for. An underlying assumption is that one will always enjoy the initiative. The operational art presupposes also that all action is always under one's positive control, even in the extremities of violence that the modern battlefield is sure to produce.

Friction—as Clausewitz defined it—will have its say, but, of course, it is acknowledged chiefly, it seems, in order to be overcome, used as a kind of theoretical straw man to prove that all eventualities have been foreseen. The operational art attempts to counteract friction chiefly by means of good planning, especially by paying close attention to the alignment of all the elements of one's own combat power in space, time, and effect—a technique ordinarily called "synchronization."[23]

Not one of these ideas was in any way original, but the way in which they were redefined, managed, and applied was new. Putting new wine in old bottles works, sometimes.

Operationalizing the Urban Campaign

As a means of expressing a particular style of war, the operational art has proved to be useful. It is better to have any concept rather than none at all, which was the state of affairs before its inception in the early 1980s.[24] Furthermore, *a concept that is completely wrong is better than no concept at all* simply because there is a chance someone will notice and attempt to correct it, to adjust toward a degree of "rightness" at least.

But we can be more generous than this. During its career, the operational art convinced the US Army that precise, integrative planning—and precisely rehearsed training—could yield favorable tactical results—results that could be anticipated, not merely hoped for. Indeed, the performance of the operational art as a means of planning and directing military action within a theater of operations has been such that one need not expect either its replacement or its revision in the foreseeable future. If the US Army is to deal with the new challenges of urbanism, therefore, it will do so within the confines of the operational art, or not at all. The operational art is here to stay.

One of the earliest proponents of the operational art, General Don Holder, has written that "theater operations fall more clearly into the domain of art than that of science. Below the level of broad principles, each situation varies so strongly in personal, geographic, demographic, historical, and economic details that the teaching of the operational art will resemble political science more than small-unit tactics."[25] Urban operations cannot be shoehorned into the operational art. If the operational art is to have any utility in this case, it must acknowledge certain realities unique to the nature, structure, and functions of such a world.

Bearing this dictum in mind, how might this knowledge be fused with knowledge of the operational art in order to "operationalize" urban campaigning? For that, we must return to the results of our earlier analysis of the urban environment, which are best considered as a set of militarily significant propositions.

First: Cities are human-built for human purposes and look and act the way they do because of this. Inevitably, some will say that, while this may be true, it is militarily irrelevant. These are the same who will say that while it is true that armies are human built for human purposes, the fact is militarily irrelevant. However, certain generalizations about cities can be made, just as certain generalizations can be made about any other shape that human aggregations take on. We may speak, for instance, of a city's morale no less reasonably than we may speak of an army's morale so that we may inform our speculations about how a city will perform under certain conditions just as we would an army or any other human aggregation. Similarly, it is not at all unreasonable to speak of a city's psychological or sociological or economic profile, just as it is reasonable to view a city in a materialistic way, as a collection of buildings, services, functions—just as we view armies materialistically, in terms of their inventories of weapons, differentiation of skills, missions, and so on. Indeed, the ways in which one may see a city, the methods by which one may analyze a city, are so extensive that no good purpose would be served here by cataloguing them; we are interested here only in those matters that are militarily important. In this instance, the most militarily significant feature of a city is its humanness. Of all facts about cities, this one is the most significant and forms the foundation of all the propositions that follow.

Next: Cities are not natural entities, in that they do not arise without human intervention upon a given natural environment. Since cities arise for the reasons of those who build them, the shape, design, and functions of a city are well within the reach of understanding, and if this is true, then cities may be analyzed on a military as well as any other basis. That is to say, an expert in transportation may analyze a city on the basis of information that is significant to his inquiry while disregarding other information that is of no significance, but the standards by which he makes these choices are choices for which he has been educated and trained. Without this education and training, his choices would be less than authoritative because they are not so much choices as guesses. In the same way, a military analysis of a city must be founded upon information that is pertinent to one's mission or tasks, and a significant part of this analysis will derive from the character of the city itself.

Next: There is no "Emerald City," shimmering on the horizon in splendid isolation. Real cities have never and do not now exist in a vacuum. Every city exists within a physical network of other cities, towns, villages, suburbs, or exurbs. Every one of these lesser aggregations defines itself at least partly by reference to the greater city, just as the greater city defines itself, at least partly, by reference to its surroundings. This dictum has tremendous importance for urban planners; it should be no less significant for military planners. The existence of greater and lesser urban zones within mutually supporting distance should alert any military analyst or planner to how forces might be disposed.

Next: Cities are not inert. Cities do not merely react; they interact. Malfunction of public systems, catastrophes, natural disasters, civic disorder, crime, riot, insurrection, or invasion and occupation—all these produce not merely a reaction in a city but an interaction. Cities are not inert because people are not inert. Military instrumentalists prefer to regard cities as inanimate material, good only for violent rearrangement. But the human and material properties of cities enable them to fight back. The potential military application of a city's human and material properties must therefore be a leading element of any military planning that involves an urban operational area.

Next: Movement, compressed in space and time, is a normal state of a city, some of whose most important functions entail the sustainment and movement of people, goods, and information. No city can be said to operate at constant velocities, but anyone knows that certain cities have certain rhythms, peculiar to themselves—the most obvious example being the rush hours. These rhythms can be managed—indeed they are managed all the time—and they can be disrupted as well. Some of these rhythms are critical to maintaining the optimum space-time distributions to which the city has become accustomed. Because these rhythms affect more or less every inhabitant (even if the person is not going anywhere), and because they can be manipulated rather easily, they are militarily significant.

Next: At a certain point in their growth, cities attain a level of complexity that is the product of human and physical synergy. That point occurs when some degree of higher management is required. One might imagine the managerial difference between a country doctor's office and a small clinic and, at succeeding levels of complexity, a hospital, and then a medical center. Urban complexity, improperly managed, can act as a centrifugal force in a city. The military significance of urban complexity is that its dysfunctional tendency can be accelerated. As in the medical network, the disruption of patient transfers from emergency sites or small clinics to higher rungs on the medical treatment ladder can accentuate stress on an urban system at a time of public crisis. To repeat, it is not only that there are more moving parts, it is that those parts are moving differently.

Next: The inherent social and material order of a city may be defined as urban cohesion, a form of cohesion no less substantial (and in many ways more substantial) than military cohesion. Urban cohesion manifests itself continuously and practically by acting as a counterweight to urban complexity—by acting as a centripetal force opposing complexity's centrifugal force. In essence, urban cohesion is attained in precisely the same way military cohesion is attained: when an individual subordinates oneself to a larger group in order to benefit less immediately but more reliably. Urban organization is made possible by this widespread social agreement. Urban cohesion and military cohesion are alike in that both can be manipulated with some degree of precision and from the tactical to the strategic range.

Next: Cities tend to persist. Contrary to what professional moralists would have us believe, cities do not exist in a state of entropy, degeneration, or decay. Cities possess adaptive capacities that often strain credulity. Toward the end of the latest battle of Grozny, Russian authorities estimated that upwards of 35,000 noncombatants had remained in a city where no buildings had escaped serious damage, where no regular services existed, and where movement was possible only at night, if then. This situation is not substantially different from the situation that existed only four years before. Cities are highly adaptive entities.

Next: Cities are built to operate in peace. The attributes and processes discussed here operate best in peace, but, as already noted, the stress of conflict does not automatically trigger degradation. Instead, the stress of conflict may lead these attributes and processes to "mobilize" themselves, as in the conversion of London's underground to public shelters during the Blitz. This is only an example of a city under attack, on the defensive, but armies have mobilized cities in order to launch attacks from them as well.

Next: A city may be divided into two parts—that which is apparent and that which is not apparent. The first consists simply of the obvious city, the city which anyone can see with an offhand glance. It is the human and material aggregation that seems to make little sense to the casual observer, but which can, with little effort, be understood as a network of human and material systems. The second consists of the invisible city, with its cybernetic signature, which presents to the casual observer the greater difficulty in understanding. But even the invisible world is quickly becoming familiar. These new ways of perceiving an urban environment will not replace the older ways; they will simply merge with one another.

Last: Assuming these propositions are generally correct, we should return to the question of military practicality posed earlier. These propositions are interesting in their own right, but that is not the same as being operationally relevant. Nor is it the same as saying that they add in any way to the military knowledge required for dealing with modern urban conflict. We need only apply a simple test: whether any of the characteristics of urbanization discussed here are beyond the reach of manipulation. Those that are beyond our reach, we may dispose of promptly; they are interesting but of little immediate use to us. Those that remain, however, are militarily relevant.

Manipulation implies that a degree of control has been imposed over a particular environment. We may envision a case in which it is considered operationally desirable to upset an urban area's balance between complexity and cohesion. An action as simple as interrupting a central power supply *at intervals* may excite an effect that, when combined with other actions, may achieve an objective. It is enough for the purpose of this example to show that one has superceded routine controls. Those who normally control this process no longer do. The attainment and sustainment of control is the first and most important signal of success that tactics send to the operational and strategic levels of war—just as the loss of control is the first signal of failure.

Having discussed certain general characteristics of a city that may be militarily significant, we are able to consider the characteristics that are unique to cities under military stress. We are not concerned so much here with the usual sorts of trouble in which cities may find themselves, such as that caused by natural or industrial catastrophe. Civil emergency systems attend to these sorts of stress, or more extensive regional emergency alliances are called out when the disaster is too big for any one city to handle. State or national military organizations may contribute to the relief effort as well. Even in such emergencies, however, the general shape, behavior, and control of the urban area remain in force. As a general rule, the critical "line of departure" between public emergency and military operation may be when duly constituted public control no longer functions. But it is the city's

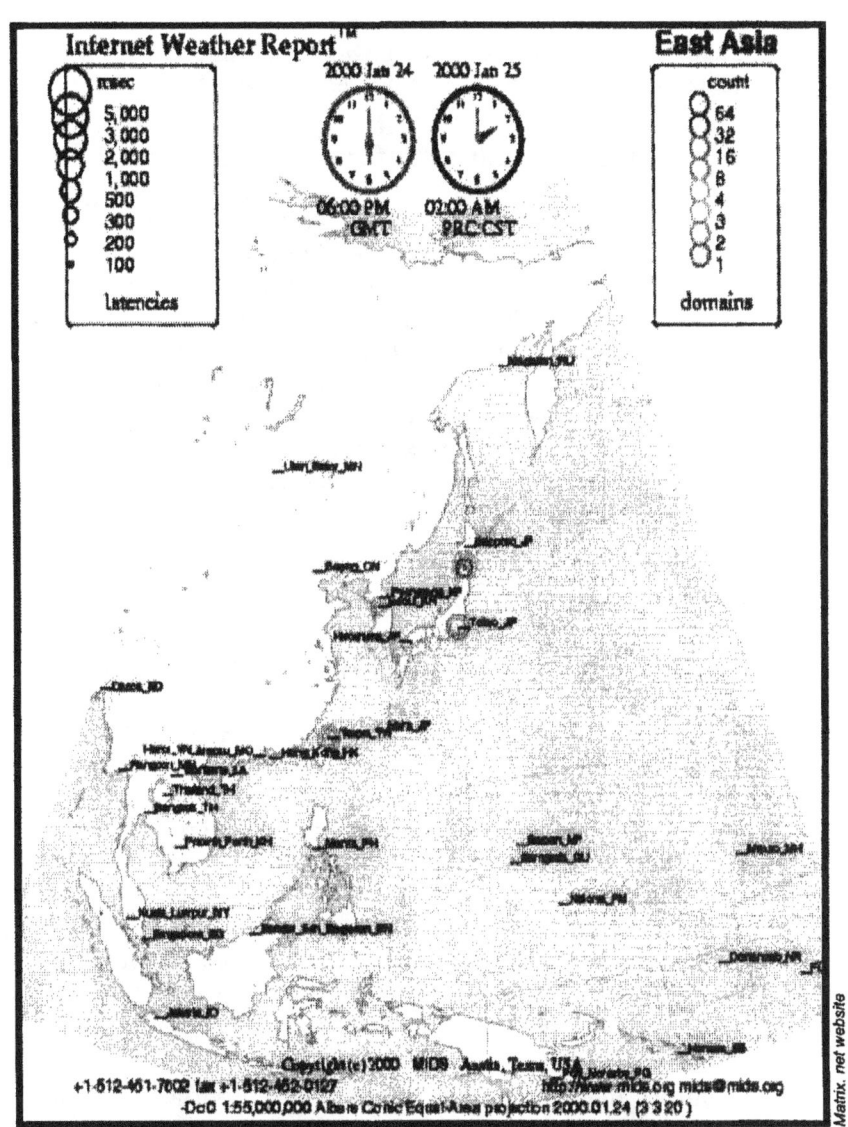

A "weather report" on the status of internet domains for East Asia, 20 January 2000

protean quality that brings us to consider its uniquely military characteristics, which can also be considered as a set of propositions:

First: Conflict militarizes a city. This may seem obvious, but the implied and real danger of conflict transforms a city so thoroughly that even local military commanders may be reluctant to rip up grand boulevards or demolish important building until it is too late. Indeed, German commanders in charge of occupied Paris in 1945 temporized their defensive operations in defiance of orders from their highest authorities. Conflict—all that it implies and entails—generates extreme stresses on any urban locality. These may be quite obvious: checkpoints and roadblocks, an increase in military traffic and a decrease in civil traffic. The normal movements of the entire city may be affected. Great avenues that carried high volumes of traffic before the conflict may be rendered entirely untenable, forcing traffic onto minor streets and, in the process, creating a vulnerable mass of people. And, of course, the most ordinary of buildings can be transformed into fortresses simply by virtue of their tactical relationship to the enemy. Other changes may be operationally important. Before the war came to Stalingrad, the primary value of the Volga River lay in its function as a great north-south axis for bulk transportation. With the onset of operations at this point of the river, the Volga became instead a great natural barrier to eastward movement. The Volga had been redefined, in effect. Perhaps we may regard these changes as obvious and straightforward, but collectively they have the power to alter an urban environment more extensively than an earthquake. The important thing to remember is that these changes do not occur "naturally" but because of military events; the changes can be either so obvious or so subtle that they will not serve as a reliable guide to the commander who is trying to understand what he is seeing. The best test, therefore, of whether a conflict has militarized an urban area is simply to ask whether military or civil authority is in control. Once that question has been answered, more exacting operational and tactical calculations can begin.

Next: Conflict internationalizes a city. After conflict in a city develops to a certain point, that city transcends its nationality and assumes a global identity. The city may be an "international" city already. Or, like Srebrinica, Mogadishu, and Grozny, the city can be quite deservedly obscure and still be elevated into global view by the conflict itself. Consider that during the Gulf War, the international press was limited to reporting mainly from Riyadh or Baghdad; yet, even under these restrictions, media operations consumed twice the available satellite bandwidth consumed by military operations. Over one hundred nations around the globe were able to receive live broadcasts simultaneously—and there was no fighting in any city.[26] In the past, armies have enjoyed certain advantages by conducting their affairs out of public view, but it is clear enough now that practically every military operation in the future will be conducted under the glare of global scrutiny. In all probability, world viewers will be treated to real-time transmissions of tactical ground combat in the not-so-distant future.

Next: Cities, for these reasons, can no longer be isolated. The advantages of "investing" a city—physically segregating it from any hope of external support—have been nullified for the most part by the information revolution. Smaller towns, villages, settlements, and the like may still be vulnerable to quarantining from their surroundings but fall into the category of the tactical small change of larger operations—that is, they produce a limited effect for the tactical investment required.

Next: In cities, the advantage rests with the defense only at the tactical level. It is strategic or operational inferiority that drives an enemy to resort to such desperate measures in the first place. The combatant that pins all his hopes on winning by tactical means what has been denied to him by strategy is really only praying that his enemy's will is too fragile to sustain a conflict. In any case, the tactical advantage of the defense is not a permanent state of affairs; naturally, the conflict decides. Certain characteristics of modern cities—such as their increasing complexity—work against even the traditional advantages of the defense. At the strategic and operational levels of an urban mission, the offense predominates, which, *inter alia*, means that an army may be able to get into trouble faster than it can get out.

All of this is why, finally, global urbanism's power to redefine strategic and operational values should be apparent, and why those values must now be addressed.

The Campaign and the City

In keeping with the traditions of their craft, professional soldiers will want to know why urbanized areas should figure in their calculations at all? After all, when ground forces find themselves in urbanized terrain, it is commonly for transient reasons—to prop up one regime or another or to sift through the wreckage of some civil disaster. It is much more difficult to imagine putting a campaign together with a city—that is, to imagine a campaign in which an urbanized area plays either a leading or a supporting, but nevertheless essential, role.

And in defense of their argument, professional soldiers often point to the Persian Gulf War. Few cities seem to have meant less to the course and conduct of a modern campaign than Kuwait City did during the Gulf War. Kuwait City was seized early on by lead Iraqi divisions in August 1990 and quickly handed over to lesser formations, who went about the business of looting the place and terrorizing the inhabitants in the time-honored ways. The lead divisions then resumed their advance toward the Saudi Arabian frontier. This was the movement that excited the formation of the allied coalition that, in the fullness of time, liberated Kuwait. The taking of the city with little or no resistance excited little. Real and invented outrages committed inside the city did not extend to foreign embassies or encroach in any way upon diplomatic niceties. The temporary internment of foreign nationals—including US citizens—did not seem sufficient in and of itself to warrant a war or even a relief expedition. There was to be no modern-day version of the Boxer expedition, no fifty-five days at Peking.

By the time American intelligence agencies deigned to believe their own senior analysts, the invasion of Kuwait seemed to be on the verge of becoming an invasion of Saudi Arabia as well. The prospect of 20 percent of the world's oil supply under the control of one warlord energized the international community with what seemed a proper *casus belli*.[27] Appropriately, then, when US Central Command's planners received guidance from their commander in chief (CINC), Kuwait City was nearly incidental to all planning considerations.[28] Kuwait City would serve as an excellent bait for deception and diversion spoofs. Postwar attempts to cast Kuwait City as a viable target for amphibious operations or as the objective for an allied main effort rather overdignifies the military significance of the place. The city's eventual liberation came about because it was uncovered by field operations far beyond its precincts not because of anything that happened inside the city. Kuwait City was a cat's-paw, nothing more.

Much the same could be said of Baghdad. Neither the city nor much of anything that happened inside of it—save nightly news reports from the roof of the Al-Rashid Hotel—was strategically important to the campaign. Unprecedentedly precise bombing, presumably intended to force the Iraqi regime to see the futility of its actions, did not.

The only other city to take on higher significance during this war was not even in the theater of operations. That was Tel Aviv. To this day, no one knows what the Iraqi regime intended to achieve by attacking Israel, notwithstanding the general speculation that it was to "divide the coalition" between those who would stand to Israel's defense and those who would not. Iraq was prevented from doing much at all by the crude technological state of its missiles, which is not to say that Iraq would have done more with better missiles. Iraq had quite a functional air force, but it did not function.

The apparent relegation of all these cities to the sideline seems to have allowed the operational art what may have been its exposition in the purest possible form: a war on a sand table. It may have been the only place in the world where such operations even could have been contemplated.

The Center of Gravity

There was plenty of national strategy but not much military strategy in the Persian Gulf War, which never quite transcended the operational level. Guidance was issued, much revised through successive iterations; planning was conducted with obsessive devotion to detail; and the reputation of this approach to war was assured until the next outing. Not then or since has there been any better concept offered as a replacement. To repeat, an obsolescing concept is better than no concept at all—but not much better.

So, interestingly, the means of achieving success was settled well before strategic success was actually defined. If there was some indecision over strategic objectives, or even operational objectives, there apparently was none about the "center of gravity." The center of gravity became a kind of Holy Grail for commanders and policymakers who did not reach any sort of strategic closure. The center of gravity was the one sure thing in a junkyard of strategic concepts: the Iraqi Republican Guard was designated by the CINC as the center of gravity. It occupied pride of place in a mission statement that went so far as to identify the precise units to be destroyed: "Attack Iraqi political-military leadership and command-and-control, gain and maintain air superiority, sever Iraqi supply lines, destroy chemical, biological, and nuclear capability, destroy Republican Guard force in the Kuwaiti Theater, liberate Kuwait."[29]

As it happened, the allies did not need to destroy the Republican Guard in order to liberate Kuwait, which leaves one wondering what really was the center of gravity after all.[30] The ease with which the war was planned and executed suggests to many that the operational design itself is more important than the elements that compose it. Some may even say that, if one does not wish a city to be relevant to a campaign, then one may simply ignore it.

Of course, this is nonsense. *A center of gravity is not something one designates but discovers.* One may imagine any number of scenarios in which the status of Kuwait City was not so incidental to operations as it was. In these cases, an operational planner would be faced with the question of whether the seizure of the city was of direct or subsidiary importance to the overall design of his operation.

Indeed, this was the very question the operational planners in the Iraqi army were required to answer at the beginning of the war. Kuwait City was critical to their plan's consummation, since Iraq's immediate strategic objective was the annexation of Kuwait. To have invaded Kuwait and declared its annexation as Iraq's "nineteenth province" without occupying Kuwait City would have been an absurdity.

The manner in which Kuwait City was taken showed no small amount of coordination and organization. Just after midnight on 2 August, three Republican Guard divisions with over 1,000 tanks crossed the frontier, making directly for the "heights" overlooking Kuwait City. Heliborne special forces assaulted the city center shortly thereafter, seizing key government installations by *coup de main*. Eleven divisions invaded Kuwaiti territory within the next four days, but Kuwait City had fallen by the evening of the first day.[31]

Of course, *coups de main* have a venerable tradition in their own right. If the invasion of Kuwait were to be translated into terms appropriate to the operational art, where would one find the center of gravity? Here, as in the US invasion of Panama the year before, the center of gravity consisted not of a place or a thing but an event: the forcible seizure of civil power by one party from another. When, at the end of Iraq's first day in Kuwait, the city was reported as secured, that meant, among other things, that no other power competed for control over the city. In other words, *the center of gravity was to be found only in the city and nowhere else.* Yet, when the allies lay their plans to overturn this state of affairs, it was not simply a matter of reversing what Iraq had done. From the allies' point of view, the solution was not to be found in Kuwait City. By then, the control of all Kuwait had passed beyond the country itself.

So, we have here, in the same war, a case in which the seizure of a city is essential to the success of a campaign, and another case in which possession of a city is incidental to the success of a campaign—and it is the same city. The city and the war interact differently in different strategic and operational cases.

On the Employment of Friction

Interaction of any sort in any environment will produce friction, and since before Clausewitz, the elimination of friction in war has been the military theorist's dream. Better, by far, to treat it as a constant presence, however, a reality to be acknowledged.

Even though friction is a constant, it does not behave uniformly for the simple reason that those things which interact are not themselves uniform. No one would mistake the friction one experiences in jungle fighting with the friction one experiences in urban fighting. The presence of an infantry squad in a jungle environment produces a different effect than one on a street corner. Not only is the friction of urban fighting different, it is more intense, and we do not have to look far for the reasons: cities function at a higher speed and more highly compressed scale. In the same way, the possibilities for interaction between that squad on the street corner and the environment in which they are operating are more numerous and more varied than their counterparts in the jungle. As it happens, the most modern armies of the world have long since acknowledged this difference by their tactical procedures, if not their operational doctrines: one need only consider tactical "rules of engagement" that have been created for various American operations in urban areas over the past several years and compare those required for use in, for example, the Persian Gulf War.

The relationship of modern armies to friction in any environment has been *defensive*, however. That is, armies have concentrated on how to minimize the negative effect of friction or somehow avoid it. No one seems to have considered the positive effects friction offers to the army that learns how to manipulate it. Friction can be employed as an offensive tool, and as the urban environment already produces friction at high levels of intensity, it stands to reason that the army that learns how to manipulate friction to the detriment of the enemy has added an important capability to its arsenal.

The larger, more populous, and more complex the city, the better the chances for employing friction in offensive fashion. In the past, a city's size and complexity were regarded as chiefly benefiting the weaker party in an urban conflict, favoring the defensive. And, indeed, recent experience would seem to uphold this generalization. But as we have seen, the character of cities is changing, and changing at a higher velocity than ever before. The offensive employment of friction is only one of those new approaches made possible by these developments. The intensity of friction is magnified many times in an urban environment, which is only another way of saying that small acts may have large consequences.

An example of how friction may be employed offensively is not difficult to imagine, for all that is really required is to establish a measure of control—and not even complete control—over a city's virtual or physical environment. Every city's power supply is automated to some degree, for instance, and the larger the city, the more demands for manipulating power at certain times and levels, since no city operates uniformly. Destroying this power supply would be relatively simple, and, in fact, that has been the usual manner of dealing with it, but we need not restrict our options to turning switches on or off. Technical and other means exist whereby control, or at least measures of system interference, can be inserted well before a conflict begins. For the purposes of military conflict, establishing the capacity to manipulate an adversary's power supply is infinitely superior merely to destroying it, for the simple reason that destruction does not offer the opportunity for control. And, to repeat, manipulation and control are the keys to achieving one's goals—unless one's goals are merely punitive in nature. In any case, the option to destroy is always available if the more technical approach fails to satisfy the requirements of one's campaign.

Establishing control over a metropolitan power supply is a relatively technical matter, and one might therefore be led to think that the offensive employment of friction applies only in higher technical realms, but this is not so. Here, we are concerned more with operational principles than with tactics, but the creation of friction may be as simple as creating barriers to traffic flow so as to channel movement in the directions required. A checkpoint or a roadblock may be useful for this purpose alone, not only for the usual reasons of population control. Checkpoints and roadblocks are established, of course, only after one's forces have entered an urban area, but if one wished to interrupt traffic flow *before* one's forces arrived, any number of means are available to effect physical changes in the urban landscape, from direct physical attack on roads to the wreckage of particular structures to impede or isolate traffic.

The difference between the friction created by direct physical means and that created by indirect, or remote, technical means may be strategically or operationally significant, however. Using high explosives against a trafficway may accomplish a limited tactical goal, but as we know, the rubble of a city can pose more hazards than benefits for the offensive in the longer term. Friction engendered by technical means promises a greater degree of precise control for a longer period than simple physical destruction. In other words, it is always better to control the whole process than a single event.

These examples fall into the world of tactics, and, anyway, the seizure of a power or water supply is hardly a novel idea. But the offensive employment of friction at the strategic or operational level turns out to be not so mysterious either. Qiao Liang and Wang Xiangsui of China's People's Liberation Army (PLA) have already described in their recent work how to create strategic friction by technical, nonmilitary means—although in their view there is "nothing in the world today that cannot become a weapon." To these two military professionals, the distinction between military and nonmilitary means has disappeared. Thus, to them, the international financier George Soros' operations in the Southeast Asian markets in 1998 constituted what they call "financial warfare." And, significantly, Liang and Xiangsui are interested in the *Aum Shinrikyo* attack in Tokyo less for its actual destruction than the disruptive terror that it created.[32]

The principle remains the same: regardless of the means employed or the specific objective sought, the purpose is to improve one's own chances of control, while defeating the enemy's control. If one is on the offensive, the enemy will be in possession of one's objectives, its systems, and its processes. Imposing friction upon the enemy places him in the position of defending a trench line against distant fires: he cannot move and can only wait for the attack.

Friction is intensified in an urban context because of what might be called the "magnification effect." We can think of a city as a magnifying lens through which every one of our actions must pass as we campaign against it, or in it. If this were all that happened, we might be satisfied to say that the process of interaction was in operation, and nothing more. But when our action passes through this magnifying glass, it is refracted: our action produces a result that is more or less what we intended, but never precisely so. The magnification effect forces upon us the necessity to adjust our subsequent actions to meet the new state of affairs. In essence, the magnification effect is responsible for the difference between what we expect of our actions and what we actually manage to do. It is also responsible for actions being more important than we think they will be when we commit them. If one were campaigning in the desert, one would be much less likely to commit a tactical act that had strategic implications than one would if operating in a city, where such chances abound.[33]

On Combat Power

The fundamental element in the creation of friction in war is physical violence, but it is a genie that soldiers long ago put in its bottle, for insensate violence is violence to no purpose. As soon as violence is harnessed to a purpose, it is under some measure of control, and the question all along has been the degree to which control is possible—the more susceptible to soldierly control violence is, the better. Then it can be a tool, not merely a force of nature. Once violence can be manipulated, the level and intensity of violence become matters for professional calculation at all the levels of war—strategic, operational, and tactical. With the advent of the operational art, the production and manipulation of combat power became an important element in the art of war beyond tactics. Now, the US doctrinal glossary defines combat power as "the total means of destructive and/or disruptive force which a Military (sic) unit/formation can apply against the opponent at a given time."[34] But this definition, in effect, demilitarizes the term, diluting the "combat" in "combat power."

In an era when scientific and technical means of waging war have outrun the use of physical force and when the employment of force is more measured and more highly controlled than ever, the modification of "combat power" as an operational idea would have happened sooner or later. Consider an early definition: "the process by which methods are selected that determine the application and utilization of combat power—the means—to achieve a desired end." Beyond the tactical level of operations, however, "combat power" is unnecessarily confining. The dimensions of *military power* have overtaken the idea that the ultimate goal is to put steel on target, especially when tactics are regarded as the realm of last resort. The commander in the field has more elements of military power at his call than elements of combat power alone. If he is operating against or within a city, he may well need all of those elements of power to accomplish his mission. If he attempts to accomplish the urban mission by combat power alone, he will likely fail.[35] Too often in conventional operations in the past, combat power—and even more specifically, firepower—has been made to compensate for shortcomings in strategic or operational vision. Yet it is clear that, in today's world, one's campaign must be well on the way to success before one's troops hit the ground. The burdens upon *combat power* must shift rearward, in the direction of *military power*, toward preparation and away from execution as the engine of the campaign.

Fusion and the Urban Campaign

The reasons a city may become involved in a given conflict are beyond counting. A city may be subverted, defended, occupied, attacked, or wrecked—or some combination thereof, partially or mostly. Concocting an operational typology only encourages the illusion that simply listing possibilities for action is the same as understanding the purposes for which the action is undertaken—precisely the opposite of how a campaign should be designed.

During the past two decades, the process of campaign design at the operational level has become well understood in the US Army, but at the same time, technological developments have underscored a tendency for the operational level and the strategic level to fuse together. Paradoxically, this trend has accelerated when American policymakers and strategists professed themselves extremely sensitive to the dangers of operational and tactical micromanagement. A telling exchange occurred during a White House press conference on the first day of Operation Just Cause when Presidential press secretary Marlin Fitzwater was asked by a reporter, "Who's got operational control?"

"Operational control is in the Pentagon," the press secretary replied.[36]

Fitzwater did not misspeak. Only two days before, the chairman of the Joint Chiefs of Staff had been revising F-117 bombing "offsets" to 250 yards for certain targets at Rio Hato.[37] The secretary of defense, pledging to himself that he would "stay out of their hair," nevertheless reviewed all the plans for the operation, including, it seemed to the chairman, those "right down to squad level."[38]

Driven by the need to justify and explain the Panama operation to the American and international public, to understand the shape of the operation in order to react to unforeseen problems, the American chain of command thoroughly violated its own policy of noninterference in field operations. In the end, these same officials would oversee the conduct of the Persian Gulf War, their experience and appetites moderated only by the much larger and more complex dimensions of that operation, and, in the end, they would congratulate themselves that they had remained true to their operational philosophy.

Yet modern strategic direction provided tools for this kind of operational oversight that were not available only a few years before. The intervening period had seen the advent of the so-called "military-technical revolution." If the tools for fusing strategic and operational direction were at hand, and if the result was a more precise application of national power, who was to say that the dead hand of history should prevent them from using those tools? During the last decade, the return to the continental United States of most forward-deployed forces, in fact, renders this a near necessity. Henceforth, American military operations abroad will be increasingly and precisely controlled from the strategic center, just as the requirement for highly controlled urban operations will come to be understood. The strategic and operational art will eventually be revised to accord with this new state of affairs.

Culmination Points, Decisive Points, Interior Lines, and Ways Ahead

The "culmination point" of an operational campaign is described in doctrinal literature as "that point in time and space when the attacker's combat power no longer exceeds that of the defender or when the defender no longer has the capability to defend successfully." Decisive points are defined as those points, not only physical, that give a commander "a marked advantage" over the enemy. Commonly, these decisive points are reached by achieving a succession of objectives, which themselves constitute a line of operations whose origin can be found at a base of operations within interior lines.[39] These definitions are sure to be useful if one intends to refight the Civil War, but as useful tools for modern American operations, their days may be numbered. Virtually every trend and development discussed in this study militates against their utility in the future. But it is one thing to declare a set of old tools less useful than they could be and quite another to find effective replacements.

Naturally, one would suspect that the scientific and technical fields that have had such an important influence in creating the present state of affairs would exercise a correspondingly important influence in the problems associated with it. No doubt, these fields have contributions to make to our understanding of the nature and conduct of urban operations—but they have not made them yet. Wargaming and simulations techniques evidently have not been able to reach into the insubstantial realms of the operational art, although they have proved themselves useful adjuncts to higher levels of training. But training,

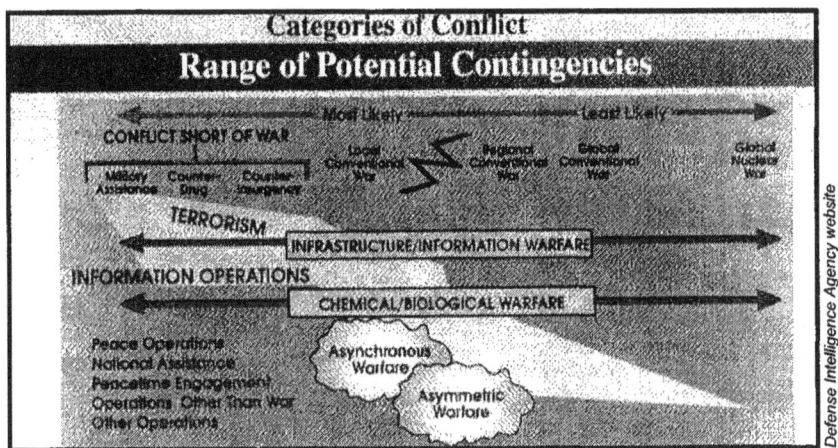

The "Full Monty"

even at the higher levels of the operational art, has its limits, fixed as it is on specific skills and straightforward operational-tactical questions. Getting at the "art" of it, as General Holder has written, is a different matter.

Turning the Sharpest Corner: Toward the "Best Available Military Thought"

Military theory is often described as nothing more or less than disciplined thinking about military affairs, and military doctrine has been defined as "the best available military thought that can be defended by reason."[40] No mind should be easily changed, especially not that of the professional soldier who has larger responsibilities. Yet no end of effort is spent telling the soldier *what* to think rather than *how* to think. Rather than specifying grand objectives for the next generation of professional soldiers, the sharpest corner of all may lie simply in putting in place the tools that will enable the soldier to see the urbanized, operational world accurately.

With one minor and recent exception, no American institution of higher military education offers instruction on urban conflict at the operational level and above. The reasons for this state of affairs should be clear to the reader by this point. These reasons are also why the chances of substantive change in the professional study of urban operations run against the odds.

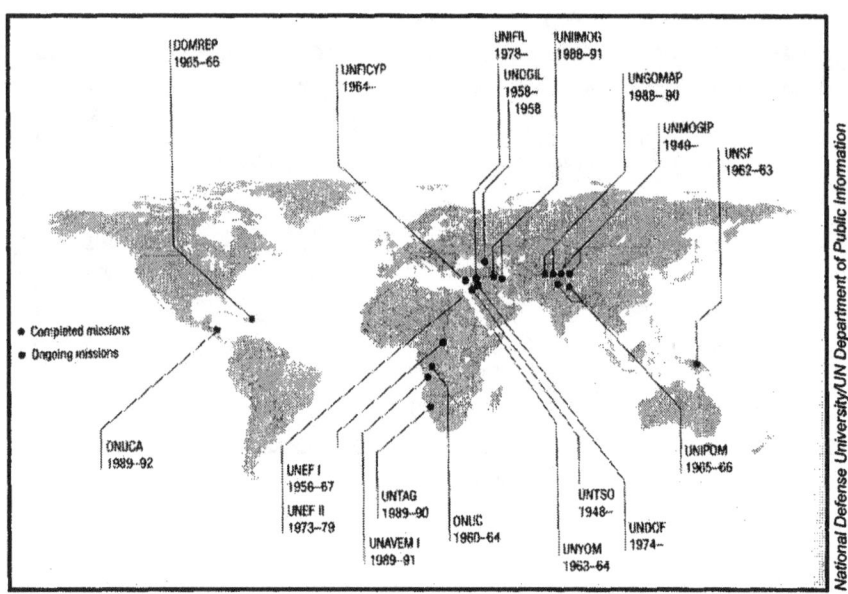

UN peace operations during the Cold War

Assume those odds might be overcome. How might the US Army prepare its field-grade and higher officers for urban operations in the future?

The first requirement for any operation is information—data. But in a world where there is a surfeit of data, where does one begin, and how does one discriminate between the data one needs to retrieve and the data one can do without for the purposes of the moment? The shelves of Army libraries the world over once groaned with a collection of "country studies" that served as a kind of "operator's dictionary" for a given nation. Contained there were general data of the sort one might find in a standard geographical reference work or encyclopedia, but specific data could be had as well—such as air and seaport "throughput capacities," communications infrastructure, and so forth. Frequently, these data were dated even before the volumes were published. Too often, however, American expeditionary planners and operators found themselves reduced to understanding their area of operations by gazing intently at an Esso map or a Michelin guide.

There is today little hope of any published form being of real assistance to operational planners or their commanders, but the appetite for operationally useful data has accelerated. There is a need for a new

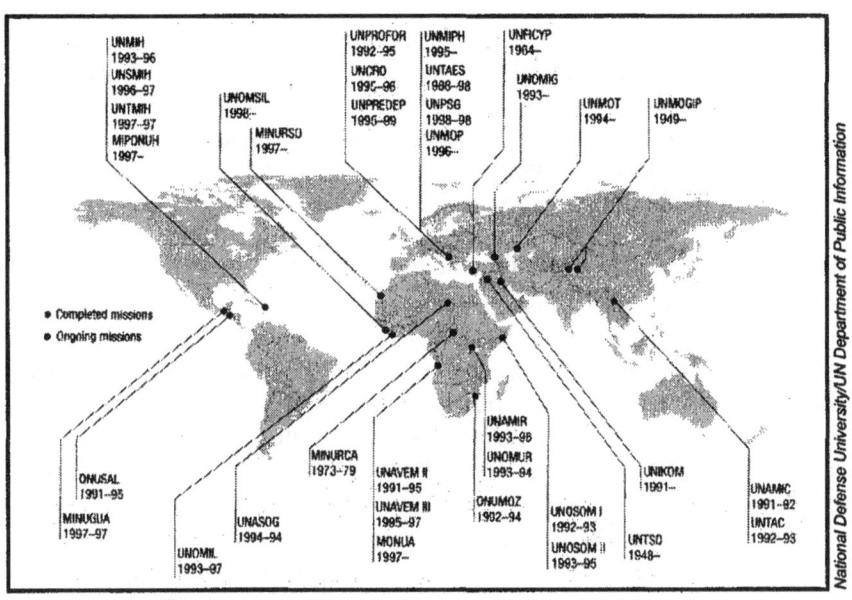

UN peace operations during and after the Cold War

form of "country study," one that consists of unrestricted sources that may be accessed by technical means from the remotest locations. Data requirements could be keyed directly to the requirements of the mission, and the need for some sort of "traveling library," which may or may not be appropriate, would be eliminated. The objective, of course, is not to have all the data, merely the data one needs.

Of course, if one has no idea of the special character of the urban environment or of campaigns conducted in it, one is bound to be hard pressed to prepare in any way. As it stands now, even the manner in which the US Army depicts military symbols for purposes of control seems hopelessly old-fashioned. How, for instance, would we depict the progress of a reconnaissance that was being conducted through a sewer system? How would we depict the progress of a fight between different floors of two different buildings, one from the sixteenth floor, another from the thirty-second floor? How could we depict a fire base that had been established on the top of an eighty-story skyscraper? No doubt we could find a way to create a new glossary of symbols fit for depicting action in the three-dimensional urban environment, but none has been found yet, as far as can be discovered.

That brings us to questions of a higher magnitude. Is it likely, for instance, that strategic or operational commanders and their planners

115

will recognize the need to break into certain of an adversary's computer systems at the earliest possible time in the arc of a campaign, or, once broken in, what contribution this might make to the success of the larger campaign? Do strategists and field commanders know the sort of systems that should be targeted, and, indeed, how those targets should be programmed to produce maximum effect—just as one programs an air tasking order? Until we can answer these questions in the affirmative, there is a more general requirement to be met.

The reason questions of technical or even nontechnical discrimination cannot be answered now is because we have no basis in accepted professional knowledge to answer them. That basis can only be reached over a longer period, perhaps as long as a generation, by a gradual process of higher professional education. The only alternative is trial and error, but the difficulty with such an approach is that someone must make an error.

Despite the probability that a majority of the soldiers in the United States Army were brought up in an urban or near-urban environment, the possibility that they will be "natural" urban fighters is rather remote. Much more likely, they will have taken this environment and their knowledge of it for granted, as a matter beneath analysis for so long that they will have difficulty seeing its inherent military possibilities. One way—not the only way but perhaps the more reliable way—to overcome such prejudices is through the medium of professional military education, where, in the company of their peers, officers would participate in experimental seminars and exercises designed to identify professional requirements for urban campaigning—in effect, creating a new branch of military knowledge that has been left behind in the military-technical developments of the last several decades.

However, it is highly unlikely that without the intervention of the Army's leadership, from the senior levels through the commandants of its many professional schools and training facilities, the US Army will undertake these reforms in the usual course of its business. Until that occurs, the institutional knowledge and experience the Army has already acquired is likely to remain hidden away. One thing is certain, however: once, the US Army would have had the alternative of ignoring the subject altogether.

Notes

1. Elaine Babcock, et al., "Conceptual Design for the Army in the Field (CONAF III): Special Study Report: Built Up Area Conflict" (Bethesda, MD: US Army Concepts Analysis Agency, 1973), 14.

2. See Robert D. Kaplan, *The Ends of the Earth: From Togo to Turkmenistan, from Iran to Cambodia—A Journey to the Frontiers of Anarchy* (New York: Vintage Books, 1996), and more seriously, Samuel Huntington, "The West, Unique Not Universal," *Foreign Affairs* 75, no. 6 (November/December 1996): 28-46. These works, only the better known of a sizable group, did much to give shape to what can only be described as post-Cold War "free floating anxiety."

3. Yahya M. Sadowski, *The Myth of Global Chaos* (Washington, D.C.: The Brookings Institution, 1998), advances the most effective critique of the "coming anarchy" school.

4. These trends are tracked most effectively through the U. S. State Department's annual reports, "Patterns of Global Terrorism," for the years 1968 through 1998. U. S. Department of State, *Patterns of Global Terrorism, 1998* (Washington, D.C.: Department of State Office of the Coordinator for Counterterrorism, April 1999), *passim*. See also Haruki Murakami, *Underground: The Tokyo Gas Attack and the Japanese Psyche*, trans., Alfred Birnbaum and Philip Gabriel (London: Harvil Books, 2000).

5. Frederick S. Dunn, Bernard Brodie, et al., eds, *The Absolute Weapon* (New York: Harcourt Brace and Co., 1946), 76. Brodie's original essay, "The Atom Bomb and American Security," written in November 1945, became the basis of his two chapters in this work. Russell Weigley, *The American Way of War* (New York: Macmillan, 1973), 367-68, wrote that Brodie's thesis amounted to nothing less than a "revolution" in American military policy. Weigley noted further that the fact of the revolution was "easier to perceive in retrospect than it was at the time."

6. Barry M. Blechman and Stephen S. Kaplan, *Force Without War: U. S. Armed Forces as a Political Instrument* (Washington, D.C.: The Brookings Institution, 1978), 38, 44, 58. This is the most authoritative accounting of Cold War expeditionary activity by the Americans. These were significant deployments. Smaller deployments to conduct routine activities, such as those of mission training teams or advisory group deployments were not regarded as particularly significant in this accounting.

7. Ibid., 44, 53.

8. Ibid., 93, 107.

9. Bob Woodward, *The Commanders* (New York: Simon and Schuster, 1992), 222-73.

10. Allen Campen, ed., *The First Information War: The Story of Communications, Computers and Intelligence Systems in the Gulf War* (Fairfax, VA: AFCEA International Press, 1992), viii, 1, 59.

11. "No evil is greater than commands of the sovereign from the court." See Sun Tzu, *The Art of War*, trans., Samuel B. Griffith, foreword by B. H. Liddell Hart (Oxford: Oxford University Press, 1963), 81.

12. Blechman and Kaplan, *Force without War*, 547-53. This is my count, taken from the author's compendium of operations.

13. Evidently, this statistic was first used in a speech at the US Army Command and General Staff College by the Chief of Staff of the Army in the fall of 1995. The speech was reprinted in *Military Review* 75, no. 5 (September/October 1995): 4-16. The statistic appears on page 7. However, inquiries by this writer have revealed no substantial data to support this statistic, which appears to have derived wholly from two slides prepared by action officers in the US Army's DCSOPS. Nevertheless, the statistic has been used and is used today as "evidence" of a heavy "OPTEMPO." The truth is that no one knows because no one has taken the trouble to do the research.

14. Barry M. Blechman, "The Intervention Dilemma," *Washington Quarterly* 18, no. 3 (Summer 1995): 63-73.

15. Ibid., 63, 66.

16. Jonathon T. Howe, "The United States and the United Nations in Somalia: The Limits of Involvement," *Washington Quarterly* 18, no. 3 (Summer 1995): 49-62.

17. See Luttwak's acerbic indictment of attrition-oriented warfare in an article that has seminal importance for the development of modern US Army doctrines, "The Operational Levels of War," *International Security* 5, no. 3 (Winter 1980/1981): 61-79.

18. See, for instance, Richard Swain's appreciation of the conduct of the war as a whole in his *Lucky War: The Third Army in Desert Storm* (Fort Leavenworth, KS: US Army Command and General Staff College Press, 1994), 71: "The popular view of the Persian Gulf War, at least in the Army, is that it was a war of maneuver. It was nothing of the sort, at least not if 'maneuver' is viewed as the psychological undermining of an enemy by movement alone."

19. Department of the Army, FM 100-5, *Operations* (1986), 14.

20. Swain, *Lucky War*, 72.

21. Ibid.

22. It is interesting to note that the Luttwak essay, cited above, mentions none of these analytical tools. My guess is that these evolved for pedagogical reasons as the Army's School of Advanced Military Studies evolved.

23. One may find these notions conveniently summarized in James Schneider's, "The Theory of the Operational Art," *Theoretical Paper No. 3* (Fort Leavenworth, KS: US Army Command and General Staff College, 1988), which is a study guide for SAMS students about to sit their comprehensive examination.

24. I categorically reject the interpretation, forwarded by some scholars, that links the inception of the operational art in the American army during the early 1980s with intellectual forbears

in the nineteenth century. Those professional officers who were most directly involved in conceiving the operational art were not in the least interested or impressed by references to classical theories or theorists. Some of these officers were thoroughly versed in classical military theory and in military history. Others, however, were not and only began their studies of these subjects when they were tasked to participate in this effort. In effect, authoritative precedents did not exist for these officers. They knew well enough that references to precedents of any kind would not impress their audience.

25. Don Holder, "Education and Training for Theater Warfare," *Military Review* (January/February 1997): 2; this essay is a reprint of an article first published in *Military Review* for September 1990, when the author was a colonel. He retired a lieutenant general.

26. Allen D. Campen, ed., *The First Information War* (Fairfax, VA: AFCEA International Press, 1992), xviii, 87.

27. Woodward, *The Commanders*, 226-29.

28. Swain, *Lucky War*, 72-73; Rick Atkinson, *Crusade: The Untold Story of the Persian Gulf War* (Boston: Houghton Mifflin, 1993), 21, 110-11.

29. Atkinson, *Crusade*, 21. As it is now well known, the state of the Republican Guard formations served as a kind of barometer for how the war in general was progressing. The destruction of half of the RG served as the decision point for the CINC on when to launch the ground campaign.

30. Furthermore, it should be pointed out that the Republican Guards were not destroyed. All that can be said for certain is that the allies applied force to some effect or set of effects that led Iraq to shift its national strategy from the offense to the defense and its military strategy from operational and tactical defense to withdrawal.

31. Ibid., 52-53. In its mechanics, the taking of Kuwait City was not unlike the United States' invasion of Panama the year before, in which 24,000 American troops attacked twenty-eight separate targets nearly simultaneously in order to overthrow the Noriega

regime. Both operations were *coups de main*, a form particularly well suited to urban missions, based on the concept of overwhelming one's enemy before he has time to react. This approach will only work if (a) one's own force is very large and well trained, (b) one's enemy is small and less well trained, and (c) the area to be covered can be smothered by your force. In Panama City as well as Kuwait City, these conditions appear to have been met.

32. Qiao Liang and Wang Xiangsui, "Unrestricted Warfare," 17, 33-34.

33. I am referring here to genuinely strategic results, not to the sort of misadventure that becomes news and gradually festers to produce a strategic movement. The strategically significant act may be newsworthy, but it does not follow that the newsworthy is always strategically significant.

34. This definition is accepted by DOD and NATO authorities and is retrieved via the US Army Center for Lessons Learned website, 20 March 2000. The US Army definition, retrieved from the same source, adds this codicil: "A combination of the effects of maneuver, firepower, protection, and leadership."

35. This passage may cause readers to think of the Russian Army's successful capture of the ruins of Grozny during the winter of 1999-2000; as this study is being written, however, it is by no means a foregone conclusion that the Russian Army will be strategically or operationally successful. "Steel on target" may have driven the rebels from their strongholds in Grozny for the moment. The issue is very much undecided, and it is not at all clear at this remove that the Russians possess the power of decision here.

36. Woodward, *The Commanders*, 184-85.

37. The targets were the PDF barracks at Rio Hato. Ibid., 177.

38. Ibid., 176. The quote is the author's paraphrase of the chairman's remarks, evidently.

39. Department of the Army, FM 100-5, *Operations*, Glossary; US Army Center for Lessons Learned website, Internet.

40. See Sir Michael Howard, "Military Science in an Age of Peace," *Journal of the Royal United Services Institution* 119 (March 1974): 3-9; for the definition of doctrine given, see the Department of the Army, *Dictionary of Terms*, 1964.

Part Four

Theory to Practice: Implications for DTLOMS

Theory to Practice

When an army's basic conceptions of warfare cannot accommodate new developments in its strategic and operational environment, several courses of action are available to it. The first—and most often preferred—is naturally to do nothing at all, in the hope that these new circumstances are only a momentary aberration, a slight arrhythmia in an otherwise healthy organ.

The second course of action is favored by the radical: this requires willfully ignoring experience and practical traditions in the name of true progress. The approach assumes that the world of the past will somehow disappear so that the new way can prevail. Unfortunately, a given point in history is never all old or all new but some mixture of the two. The US Army implicitly recognizes this when certain older "legacy" systems are referred to, meaning that they will have to stay in service just a while longer, until successor systems arrive to take their place.

The third course of action is the course taken most often: this entails a clear-headed and unsentimental view of how far the new course will diverge from the old. Then, the question becomes how much newness the institution can accommodate at a given time.

It will be said that these are the habits of a highly conservative organization, but there are excellent reasons for this inherent conservatism, which will be familiar to anyone with even the sketchiest knowledge of the history of war. Armies are conservative because they must be prepared to conserve themselves against political, technical, and operational stresses. In modern terms, armies concern themselves with readiness to perform their strategic missions. But the US Army has shown itself, on occasion, to be sufficiently flexible to handle what amounted to radical change, albeit at a pace that surely would not satisfy the most impatient transformationists among us.

If one were to compare the US Army's receptiveness toward progress with that of other armies of the world, one might be impressed to learn that the American Army has intentionally reformed itself on two separate occasions—the far-reaching Root Reforms after the Spanish-American War and the DePuy Revolution in the middle 1970s. Only a few select armies may claim to have performed such a feat. Self-reform is possible for any army. One might even argue that, in the most advanced armies of the day, regeneration may only be possible from within because of the professional-technical nature of modern warfare.

Once an army begins its regeneration, the process of change tends to flow along well-traveled institutional lines: its chain of command, its organizational networks, its professional cliques, just to name a few. Within any army, the avenues of change are not only those that are duly constituted and authorized, for we must remember that armies are distinct types of subculture as well. Any change an army undertakes must pass muster, and the number of ways an army can refuse to cooperate with reform is beyond counting. If the army does not sign up for change, the party should be canceled.

During the late 1980s, General Carl Vuono, then the US Army's Chief of Staff, began referring to several operational and institutional priorities that could keep the Army focused on its most important responsibilities. In their original shape, these priorities were doctrine, organization, training, leader development, materiel, and soldiers—or DTLOMS, for short. In the ten years and more since their inception, these priorities have come to exercise a certain discipline over the whole process of developing forces for the Army. Today, through the Army's Force Development Process, a highly formalized sequence of analyses is conducted to identify and validate specific requirements for the Army's use.

When DTLOMS made its first appearance, the strategic and operational context in which the Army operated was far different. In those days, of course, the most important strategic point of reference was the Cold War. Gradually, the Army has acknowledged that the strategic and operational verities of the Cold War are no longer in force. In 1994, the Training and Doctrine Command published its pamphlet 525-5, entitled *Force XXI Operations: A Concept for the Evolution of Full-Dimension Operations for the Strategic Army of the Early Twenty-First Century*. The concept attempted to anticipate the broader features of the Army's operational future, predicting smaller, more highly technical, more quickly and easily deployable lethal forces. Its authors wrote of a "living doctrine" based on a "fluid strategic environment"—hardly concepts the US Army would have been comfortable with just a decade earlier.[1] The newest edition of the

Army's capstone operational manual—what was once designated FM 100-5 but, to emphasize the Army's commitment to joint operations, is now Field Manual 3.0—as of this writing has been released only as a Student Text. FM 3.0 is even less tentative about the new operational style imagined in the old TRADOC concept.[2]

All of which is why it is necessary to return for a moment to the conception of war broached in the last chapter, for it is a nation's conception of war that, in the final analysis, determines the shape of an army's doctrine. If one were to enumerate the fundamental structural elements of the American conception of war in the present and foreseeable future, one would see the following:

- A US-based force.
- A standing, ready, operational force.
- A rapidly deployable strategic force.
- A technologically advanced force.
- A light force.
- A lethal force.
- A limited force.

The resulting picture is that of an American strategic expeditionary force, one whose methods naturally capitalize upon its unique character. Such a force is obviously not fitted to conduct a sustained high-intensity conflict by itself, but then, modern armies are no longer expected to operate in isolation from air and naval services, nor, indeed, is it at all probable that nations in the future would engage unilaterally in such a conflict. It is therefore no risk at all to expect that future conflict will be of the sort where forces such as those fielded now by the US Army are more than equal to operational demands. Nor is it a risk to suppose that those demands will increasingly be made and met in the urban environment.

This is the nexus—the crossroads between conflict and the urban future—where strategic questions of the future will be posed and answered.

The era of the iron force is over. The nation that will lead the military world this next century already produces and employs its coercive power differently from any army in history. Finesse is replacing weight as the basis of American military power. In times past, military force produced action by the application of weight as much as violence. Operational and tactical successes were achieved as the struggle between two masses "developed the situation." Now, the situation can be developed in advance of military action by the rapid planning and projection of national power before one soldier has deployed. The employment of cybernetic and other special, national-level assets can begin to shape the situation even before actual forces have begun to move. In the best possible case, then, the closure of friendly troops on the objective would mark the *consummation* of strategic success, not the commencement of struggle toward it. The concentration of action, time, and space in the urban environment works to the advantage of such forces, employing highly controlled, measured applications of power to achieve strategic ends in the shortest possible time. None of this has to do merely with the preference of one operational style over another; *the United States' coercive power must be applied in such a way that it attains its objectives first, even if it cannot initiate the conflict. Strategic speed is now the basis of American military power.*[3]

Requirements for DTLOMS: An Unconstrained Analysis

The translation of military theory into military practice is not so mysterious or difficult as it is usually depicted. In general, it consists merely of stating the best, or ideal, case with the knowledge that at some point practicalities will intervene, that compromises with present or unforeseen factors will have to be made, and that, in the end, some degree less than the ideal will be attained. Any idea that survives this process is more likely to be workable than not. Doctrine is the medium in which this translation is made, and that is why it is necessary to begin there.

Doctrine

The 1964 *Dictionary of Army Terms* defines doctrine as the "best available military thought that can be defended by reason." Using this basic standard, the US Army's operational doctrine with regard to full-spectrum urban operations is inadequate. In this respect, current operational doctrine merely reflects the current state of thinking on this subject in the armed forces. The same is true of subordinate tactical, or "how to fight," doctrine found in Field Manual 90-10 and FM 90-10-1. Army urban operations doctrine is, in effect, frozen in time. In light of these facts, the following changes should be considered:

- TRADOC should take the initiative in building up a new body of professional information and developing new operational-level techniques and procedures through an iterative process of general officer review boards, Battle Command Exercises, and a program designed to develop adequate simulations at higher-than-tactical level. Program development and overwatch should be conducted by a General Officer Task Group at TRADOC Headquarters.

- In conjunction and coordination with the TRADOC initiative, HQDA, DCSOPS, should establish a corresponding initiative, centered on the Army War College (AWC), whose purpose would be to address urban operations at the strategic, national, and multinational levels.

- In an initiative to be discussed more fully under the heading of Leader Development, a program of basic research and development should be established at selected TRADOC schools and coordinated by CGSC, the purpose of which would be to contribute both raw and processed data to the doctrine development process.

Training

- In conjunction with the initiatives described above, a program of command and staff exercises should be established in which commanders and their staffs from battalion to division level conduct on-site tactical exercises without troops (TEWTS) at a succession of CONUS cities selected to represent an ascending scale of size, configuration, and complexity. Operational lessons learned (ORLL) from these exercises should be collected for integration with corresponding programs and exercises.

- Battle Command Training Program (BCTP) exercises for urban operations at the operational level and higher should be developed.

- Current training at the Combat Training Centers (CTCs) should not be interrupted or altered until TRADOC validates changes by standing procedures.

Leader Development

- TRADOC should initiate a sequential and progressive program of professional-level education bearing upon the conduct of urban operations. CGSC should take the lead in developing a series of professional-level courses for resident and distance classes, the objective of which would be the establishment of a living laboratory for the advancement of professional knowledge bearing upon modern urban operations. These efforts should be coordinated with and participate in both TEWT and BCTP exercises.

- TRADOC should cooperate with HQDA, DCSOPS, and AWC in order to establish corresponding exercise events at the strategic and multinational levels.

- In addition to the developments outlined above, both institutional and unit-level programs should be initiated, the objective of which would be the basic education of Army leaders in urban operations so that professional training and education for urban operations is made an integral part of an officer's professional progress, and not merely a training event.

Organizations and Materiel

- Until such time as positive control over activities relating to urban operations can be established by the general officer task group discussed above, a moratorium should be declared on the creation of any new organizations or materiel development.

- At the same time, a TRADOC-level study should be initiated in order to capitalize upon work already in progress under the direction of TRADOC ADCST-Transition.

- Once TRADOC establishes oversight, all decisions regarding necessary changes in organization and materiel should be made according to standing procedures.

- TRADOC should convene a study group, either a stand-alone one or as part of other on-going initiatives, whose mission is to devise future organization and operational requirements for strategically deployable formations as described in this study.

Soldiers

- TRADOC should sponsor the establishment of a command-level task force whose objective is to study, analyze, and forecast psychological, physical, organizational, and material requirements unique to the individual soldier's role in twenty-first century urban operations and to ensure the integration of findings across the spectrum of DTLOMS.

In summary, it should be emphasized that these recommendations are based on the general principle that future urban operations can no longer be regarded as the exclusive province of a particular branch or activity within the US Army. Further, if the Army acts within the spirit of Joint Vision 2010, every effort must be made to capitalize upon the professional knowledge readily available within the sister services who will also be participating in any American military operation in the future.

Finally, if this study contributes in any way to an improvement in the US Army's capability to meet the challenges posed by the most probable kind of military operation in the foreseeable future, the effort and time expended will have been worthwhile.

Notes

1. *Force XXI Operations: A Concept for the Evolution of Full-Dimension Operations for the Strategic Army of the Early Twenty-First Century,* typescript pamphlet (Fortress Monroe, VA: Department of the Army, Headquarters, Training and Doctrine Command, 1 August 1994). See especially p. 4-2.

2. As of this writing, the newest edition of Field Manual 3.0, *Operations,* has not been officially released for use and may not be directly cited.

3. "Strategic Speed," as the term is used here, is meant to indicate the relative speed with which the party in a given conflict is capable of attaining its strategic objective.

Appendix:
Catalog of Selected Urban Battles

Date	City	Objective	Result	City Type
1184 BC	Troy	Conquest	Siege	Fortified city
614 BC	Jerusalem	Conquest	Sack	Fortified city
612 BC	Nineva	Conquest	Sack	Ancient walled city
612 BC	Samara	Conquest	Sack	Ancient walled city
585 BC	Tyre	Conquest	Siege	Fortified port
539 BC	Babylon	Reconquest	Occupation	Ancient walled city
494 BC	Miletus	Conquest	Siege	Ancient walled city
479 BC	Athens	Conquest	Occupation	Ancient port city
460 BC	Memphis	Insurrection	Relief of siege	Ancient port city
429 BC	Plataea	Conquest	Siege & countersiege	Fortified city
422 BC	Amphipolis	Conquest	Siege & relief	Fortified port
415 BC	Syracuse	Conquest	Siege	Fortified port
404 BC	Athens	Conquest	Siege	Fortified port
394 BC	Corinth	Conquest	Occupation	Fortified port
332 BC	Tyre	Conquest	Siege	Fortified port
332 BC	Gaza	Conquest	Siege	Fortified port
305 BC	Rhodes	Conquest	Siege	Fortified port
344 BC	Syracuse	Conquest	Siege	Fortified port
311 BC	Syracuse	Conquest	Siege	Fortified port
405 BC	Veii	Conquest	Siege	Fortified outpost
390 BC	Rome	Invasion	Occupation	Ancient city
146 BC	Carthage	Invasion	Destruction	Ancient port city
52 BC	Alesia	Invasion	Pacification	Armed camp
49 BC	Massilia (Marseilles)	Invasion	Siege	Ancient port
48 BC	Dyrrhachium	Campaign	Siege	Armed camp
48 BC	Alexandria	Relief	Countersiege	Ancient port city
AD 410	Rome	Conquest		Fortified city
451	Orleans	Conquest		Medieval city
455	Rome	Conquest		Fortified city
490	Ravena	Conquest		
717	Constantinople	Siege		Fortified city
728	Ravena	Siege		

Catalog of Selected Urban Battles (continued)

Date	City	Objective	Result	City Type
732	Poitiers	Invasion	Battle	Fortified city
752	Ravena	Siege		
754	Ravena	Siege		
756	Ravena	Siege		
885	Paris	Siege		Fortified city
1083	Rome	Conquest	Siege	Fortified city
1084	Antioch	Conquest	Siege	Walled city
1097	Antioch	Conquest	Siege	Walled city
1098	Antioch	Reconquest	Siege	Walled city
1099	Jerusalem	Conquest	Siege	Fortified city
1189	Acre	Conquest	Siege	Fortified city
1202	Constantinople	Invasion	Siege	Fortified city
1244	Jerusalem	Reconquest	Siege	Fortified city
1346	Calais	Invasion	Siege	Fortified city
1314	Stirling	Campaign	Siege/countersiege	Medieval city
1370	Limoges	Conquest	Sack	Medieval city
1401	Baghdad	Invasion	Massacre	Ancient
1418	Paris	Invasion	Massacre	Fortified city
1419	Prague	Campaign	Siege	Fortified city
1420	Paris	Relief	Siege	Fortified city
1429	Orleans	Invasion	Siege/ Relief	Medieval city
1429	Paris	Relief	Countersiege	Fortified city
1436	Paris	Relief	Countersiege	Fortified city
1453	Constantinople	Conquest	Bombardment	Fortified city
1456	Belgrade	"	"	"
1487	Malaga	Reconquest	Siege	Medieval city
1491	Grenada	Reconquest	Siege	Moorish city
1521	Milan	Invasion	Siezure	Medieval city
1521	Tenochtitlan	Invasion	Siege	Meso-american city
1521	Metz, Verdun	Invasion	Capture	Medieval cities
1524	Pavia	Invasion	Siege	Medieval city
1529	Vienna	Invasion	Siege	Medieval city
1544	Boulogne	Invasion	Siege-relief	Medieval port
1552	Metz	Invasion	Siege	Fortified city
1558	Calais	Invasion	Siege	Medieval port

Catalog of Selected Urban Battles (continued)

Date	City	Objective	Result	City Type
1569	Poitiers	Conquest	Siege	Medieval city
1609	Smolensk	Invasion	Siege	Medieval city
1614	Pskov	Invasion	Siege	Medieval city
1614	Osaka	Civil War	Siege	Fortified Asian city
1618	Pilsen	Invasion	Siezure	Medieval city
1622	Bergen-op-Zoom	Campaign	Siege	Fortified coast city
1622	Heidelberg	Campaign	Seizure	Medieval city
1623	Baghdad	Invasion	Siege	Ancient city
1627	La Rochelle	Campaign	Siege	Fortified city
1628	Stralsund	Campaign	Siege	Medieval port
1630	Magdeburg	Campaign	Siege	Medieval city
1631	Frankfurt on der Oder	Campaign	Siege	Medieval city
1632	Smolensk	Campaign	Siege & battle	Medieval city
1639	Thionville	Campaign	Siege	Fortified city
1642	Leipzig	Invasion	Siege	Medieval city
1643	Rocroi	Invasion	Siege	Medieval city
1644	York	Civil War	Siege	Medieval city
1645	Leicester	Civil War	Battle	Medieval city
1645	Freiburg	Campaign	Siege	Medieval city
1648	Colchester	Revolt	Refuge	Medieval city
1656	Riga	Revolt	Siege	Medieval port
1658	Dunkirk	Invasion	Siege	Medieval port
1673	Maastricht	Invasion	Siege	Medieval port
1683	Vienna	Invasion	Siege	Medieval city
1686	Buda	Invasion	Siege	Medieval city
1687	Belgrade	Recapture	Siege	Medieval city
1690	Belgrade	Recapture	Siege	Medieval city
1691	Mons	Invasion	Stormed	Medieval city
1692	Namur	Invasion	Siege	Medieval city
1695	Namur	Invasion	Siege	Medieval city
1701	Riga	Relief	Siege	Medieval port
1704	Gibraltar	Reconquest	Siege	Fortified port
1705	Barcelona	Reconquest	Siege	Medieval port
1706	Toulon	Campaign	Blockade	Medieval port

Catalog of Selected Urban Battles (continued)

Date	City	Objective	Result	City Type
1707	Madrid	Invasion	Siezure	Medieval city
1708	Lille		Siege	Medieval city
1709	Poltava	Invasion	Siege	Medieval city
1709	Mons		Siege	Medieval city
1716	Temesvar	Invasion	Siege	Medieval town
1717	Belgrade	Reconquest	Siege & battle	Medieval city
1745	Fort Louisbourg	Invasion	Siege	Fortified port
1751	Arcot	Suppression	Capture	Ancient city
1755	Syriam	Suppression	Siege	Ancient city
1756	Calcutta	Suppression	Capture	Ancient city
1756	Pegu	Suppression	Siege	Ancient city
1775	Boston	Suppression	Investment	Port city
1780	Charleston	Suppression	Siege	Port city
1781	Yorktown	Reconquest	Countersiege	Fortified port city
1805	Bhurtpore	Conquest	Occupation	Ancient port
1807	Danzig	Rebellion	Siege	Fortified port city
1808	Saragossa	Invasion	Siege	Medieval city
1809	Cadiz	Invasion	Occupation	Medieval port
1812	Moscow	Invasion	Occupation	Medieval city
1812	Belgrade	Rebellion	Occupation	Medieval city
1813	Dresden	Invasion	Battle	Medieval city
1813	Washington	Invasion	Occupation	River town
1814	Leipzig	Invasion	Battle	Medieval city
1815	Tolouse	Invasion	Blockade & siezure	Medieval port
1825	Athens	Insurrection	Occupation	Ancient city
1830	Brussels	Insurrection	Occupation	Occupation
1830	Antwerp		Siege	Medieval port
1830	Warsaw			Medieval city
1830	Algiers	Conquest	Capture	Ancient port
1832	Acre, Damascus, Aleppo	Invasion	Siezure	Ancient cities
1841	Kabul	Insurrection	Occupation	Ancient city
1848	Paris	Insurrection	Occupation	Medieval city
1848	Vienna	Insurrection	Occupation	Medieval city
1848	Berlin	Insurrection	Occupation	Medieval city

Catalog of Selected Urban Battles (continued)

Date	City	Objective	Result	City Type
1849	Rome	Insurrection	Occupation	Ancient city
1850	Venice	Insurrection	Occupation	Ancient port
1854	Sebastopol	Campaign	Siege	Fortified port
1863	Vicksburg	Campaign	Siege & battle	Fortified town
1863	Charleston	Campaign	Siege	Fortified port
1863	Chattanooga	Campaign	Siege & battle	River port
1870	Paris	Campaign	Siege	Medieval city
1871	Paris	Insurrection	Occupation	Medieval city
1878	Plevna	Campaign	Siege	Fortified city
1884	Khartoum	Revolt	Siege	Ancient city
1899	Mafeking	Campaign	Siege	Outpost
1900	Paardeberg	Campaign	Siege	Outpost
1904	Port Arthur	Campaign	Siege	Fortified port
1912	Constantinople	Invasion	Siege	Ancient fortified port
1913	Adrianople	Invasion	Siege	Ancient city
1914	Przemsyl	Campaign	Siege	Defended city
1916	Verdun	Campaign	Siege & battles	Fortified city
1917	Petrograd	Insurrection	Occupation	Fortified port
1918	Kiev	"	"	Medieval city
1920	Warsaw	Invasion	Occupation	Medieval city
1927	Nanchang	Insurrection		Asian metropolis
1927	Canton	Insurrection		Ancient port
1932	Shanghai	Invasion	Occupation	Ancient port
1936	Madrid	Insurrection	Siege & battles	Medieval city
1937	Shanghai	Invasion	Occupation	Ancient port
1937	Nanking	Invasion	Occupation	Ancient river port
1940	Oslo	Invasion	Occupation	Ancient port
1941	Leningrad	Invasion	Siege	Fortified port
1941	Shanghai	Invasion	Occupation	Ancient port
1941	Hong Kong	Invasion	Occupation	Ancient port
1942	Singapore	Invasion	Occupation	Ancient port
1942	Stalingrad	Invasion	Siege & countersiege	River city
1944	Myitkyina	Invasion	Liberation	Asian river city
1944	Imphal-Kohima	Invasion	Liberation	Mountain city
1944	Cherbourg	Invasion	Liberation	Fortified port

Catalog of Selected Urban Battles (continued)

Date	City	Objective	Result	City Type
1944	Paris	Insurrection	Liberation	Medieval city
1944	Antwerp	Campaign	Liberation	Medieval port
1944	Aachen	Campaign	Liberation	Medieval city
1944	Warsaw	Insurrection	Liberation	Medieval city
1945	Berlin	Campaign	Occupation	Medieval city
1945	Manila	Reconquest	Liberation	Ancient port
1947	Hue	Campaign	Occupation	Ancient capitol
1948	Jerusalem	Campaign	Occupation	Ancient city
1950	Seoul	Invasion	Occupation	Ancient city
1951	Seoul	Reconquest	Liberation	Ancient city
1958	Beirut	Intervention	Peacekeeping	Ancient port
1965	Santo Domingo	Intervention	Peacekeeping	Colonial port
1968	Saigon	Campaign	Occupation	Colonial capitol
1968	Hue	Campaign	Occupation	Ancient capitol
1972	Quang Tri	Campaign	Occupation	Market city
1973	Phnom Penh	Campaign	Siege	Ancient capitol
1975	Dublin	Insurrection	Guerrilla action	Medieval city
1979	Kabul	Campaign	Coup de main	Ancient city
1980	Kabul	Insurrection	Guerrilla action	Ancient city
1982	Beirut	Invasion	Siege	Ancient port
1988	Panama City	Invasion	Coup de main	Colonial port
1993	Mogadishu	Intervention	Stabilization	Colonial port
1994	Port au Prince	Intervention	Stabilization	Colonial port
1994	Grozny	Reconquest	Occupation	Ancient town
1999	Grozny	Reconquest	Occupation	Ancient town

Select Bibliography

Ashworth, Gregory. *War and the City*. London: Routledge, 1991.

Beevor, Antony. *Stalingrad: The Fateful Siege: 1942-1943*. New York: Viking Press, 1998.

Bell, J. Bowyer. *Besieged: Seven Cities Under Siege*. New York: Chilton Publishers, 1966.

Blood, Christopher G., and Marlisa E. Anderson. "The Battle for Hue: Casualty and Disease Rates During Urban Warfare." San Diego, CA: Naval Health Research Center, 1993.

Braudel, Fernand. *The Structures of Everyday Life*. Vol. I, *Civilization and Capitalism, 15th to the 18th Century*. Translation by Sian Reynolds. New York: Harper and Row, 1981.

──────── . *The Identity of France*. Vol. I, *History and Environment*. Translated by Sian Reynolds. New York: Harper & Row, 1990.

Briggs, Asa, and Daniel Snowman, eds. *Fins de Siecle*. New Haven, CT: Yale University Press, 1996.

Builder, Carl, and Brian Nichiporuk. *Information Technologies and the Future of Land Warfare*. Santa Monica, CA: The Rand Corporation, 1994.

Buruma, Ian. *Behind the Mask*. New York: Ballantine Books, 1984.

Chandler, Tercius, and Gerald Fox. *3000 Years of Urban Growth*. With a foreword by Lewis Mumford. New York and London: Academic Press, 1974.

Clausewitz, Carl von. *On War*. Edited and translated by Michael Howard and Peter Paret. New York: Everyman's Library, 1993.

Cohen, Eliot A. "A Revolution in Warfare." *Foreign Affairs* 75, no. 2 (March-April 1996): 37-54.

Contamine, Philippe. *War in the Middle Ages*. Translated by Michael Jones. London: Basil Blackwell, 1984.

Cranz, Donald. "Strongpoints in a Defense Against Blitzkrieg: Potential and Problems in Perspective." Fort Leavenworth, KS: School of Advanced Military Studies, monograph, 1989.

Crawshaw, Mike, ed. "Urban Warfare." SMI Conference Proceedings, 3-4 November 1999, London, England, DRAFT.

Crichton, Michael. *Rising Sun*. New York: Ballantine Books, 1992.

Crystal, David, ed. *The Cambridge Factfinder*. 3d Edition. Cambridge, MA: Cambridge University Press, 1998.

Dewar, Michael. *War in the Streets: The Story of Urban Combat from Calais to Khafji*. London: David & Charles, 1992.

Dower, John. *Embracing Defeat: Japan in the Wake of World War II*. New York: W. W. Norton, 1999.

Dupuy, R. Ernest, and Trevor N. Dupuy. *Encyclopedia of Military History from 3500 B.C. to the Present*. New York: Harper & Row, 1970.

Dutt, Ashok K. "Calcutta." In *Microsoft Encarta Encyclopedia 99*, pp. 5 and 8, CD-ROM.

Ellefson, Richard. "Military Operations in Built-Up Areas: Morphological and Functional Characteristics of Built-Up Urban Areas." Technical Report No: 4, 10 March 1974. Arlington, VA: DARPA, 1973.

Erickson, John. *The Road to Stalingrad: Stalin's War Against Germany*. Vol. I. New York: Harper and Row, 1975.

Everson, Robert E. "Standing at the Gates of the City: Operational Level Actions and Urban Warfare." Fort Leavenworth, KS: U.S. Army School of Advanced Military Studies, monograph, 1995.

Fallows, James. *Looking at the Sun: The Rise of the Near East Asian Economic and Political System*. New York: Vintage Books, 1994.

Fishman, Robert. *Bourgeois Utopias: The Rise and Fall of Suburbia*. New York: Basic Books, 1987.

Freedman, Lawrence, and John Saunders, eds. *Population Change and European Security*. London: Brassey's UK, 1991.

Geyer, Michael. "German Strategy in the Age of Machine Warfare, 1914-1945." In *Makers of Modern Strategy*. Edited by Peter Paret. Princeton, NJ: Princeton University Press, 1986.

Glenn, Russell W. *Marching Under Darkening Skies: The American Military and the Impending Urban Operations Threat*. Santa Monica, CA: The Rand Corporation, 1998.

Glenn, Russell W., ed. *Denying the Widow-Maker: Summary of Proceedings of the Rand-DBBL Conference on Military Operations on Urbanized Terrain.* Santa Monica, CA: Rand Corporation, 1998.

Glenn, Russell W. *Combat in Hell: A Consideration of Constrained Urban Warfare.* Santa Monica, CA: The Rand Corporation, 1996.

Glenn, Russell, ed. "The City's Many Faces: Proceedings of the Arroyo Center/Marine Corps Warfighting Lab/ J8 Working Group Conference on Joint Urban Operations, July 1999." Santa Monica, CA: The Rand Corporation, 1999, DRAFT.

Goligowski, Steven. "Operational Art and Military Operations on Urbanized Terrain." Fort Leavenworth, KS: U.S. Army School of Advanced Military Studies, monograph, 1995.

Goralski, Robert. *World War II Almanac: A Political and Military Record.* New York: G. P. Putnam's Sons, 1981.

Graeub, William C. "Public Transportation." In *Microsoft Encarta Encyclopedia 99.* CD-ROM.

Grant, Ulysses S. *Memoirs and Selected Letters.* New York: The Library of America, 1990.

Hall, Sir Peter. *Cities in Civilization.* New York: Pantheon, 1999.

Hong Kong Trade Development Council. "Hong Kong & China Economics, 11 January 2000." <www.tdc.org.hk/main/economic.htm>.

Horne, Alistair. *A Savage War of Peace: Algeria, 1954-1962.* New York: Penguin Books, 1977.

Howard, Michael. *The Franco-Prussian War.* London: Methuen, 1961.

Howard, Michael, William Roger Louis, and William Roger, eds. *The Oxford History of the Twentieth Century.* New York: Oxford University Press, 1998.

Hughes, Patrick M. "Global Threat and Challenges: The Decades Ahead." Washington, D. C.: Association of the United States Army Institute of Land Warfare, March 1999.

Huntington, Samuel. "The West, Unique Not Universal." *Foreign Affairs* 75, no. 6 (November-December 1996): 28-46.

James, William T. "From Siege to Surgical: The Evolution of Urban Combat from WWII to the Present and Its Effect on Current Doctrine." Fort Leavenworth, KS: U.S. Army Command and General Staff College, Master of Military Arts and Sciences, thesis, 1998.

Jordan, David P. *Transforming Paris: The Life and Labors of Baron Hausmann* . Chicago: University of Chicago Press, 1995.

Kaplan, Robert D. *An Empire Wilderness: Travels into America's Future.* New York: Random House, 1999.

Kaplan, Robert D. *Balkan Ghosts: A Journey Through History*. New York: St. Martin's Press, 1993.

Keegan, John, "Please, Mr. Blair, never take such a risk again." *London Daily Telegraph*, 6 June 1999.

Kent, Robert B. "Rio de Janeiro." In *Microsoft Encarta Encyclopedia 99*. CD-ROM.

Kern, Paul Bentley. *Ancient Siege Warfare*. London: Souvenir Press, 1999.

Kostof, Spiro. *The City Shaped: Urban Patterns and Meanings Through History*. London: Thames and Hudson, 1999.

Kostof, Spiro. *The City Assembled: The Elements of Urban Form Throughout History*. Boston: Little Brown, 1999.

Kroynenburg, Matt Van. "The Urban Century: Developing World Urban Trends and Possible Factors Affecting Military Operations." Quantico, VA: Marine Corps Intelligence Agency, Document MCIA-1586-003-97.

LaFeber, Walter. *The Clash: U. S.-Japanese Relations Throughout History*. New York: W. W. Norton, 1997.

Luttwak, Edward N. "Toward Post-Heroic Warfare." *Foreign Affairs* 74, no. 3 (May-June 1995): 109-22.

Matthews, Lloyd, ed. *Challenging the United States Symmetrically and Asymmetrically: Can America Be Defeated?* Carlisle Barracks, PA: U.S. Army War College, 1998.

McEnery, Kevin, T. "The XIV Corps and the Battle for Manila, Feb 1945." Fort Leavenworth, KS: U.S. Army Command and General Staff College, Master of Military Arts and Sciences thesis, 1993.

McLaurin, R. D., and R. Miller. "Urban Counterinsurgency: Case Studies and Implications for U.S. Military Forces." Aberdeen Proving Ground, MD: U.S. Army Human Engineering Laboratory, 1989.

McLaurin, R. D. "The Battle of Sidon." Aberdeen Proving Ground, MD: U.S. Army Human Engineering Laboratory, 1989.

_____. R. D. "Military Forces in Urban Antiterrorism." Aberdeen U.S. Army Human Engineering Laboratory, 1989.

McNeill, William H. "Demography and Urbanization." In *Oxford History of the 20th Century*. Edited by Michael Howard and William Roger Louis. New York: Oxford University Press, 1999.

Mumford, Lewis. *The City in History*. New York: MFJ Books, 1961.

Nelson, Howard J. "Los Angeles." In *Microsoft Encarta Encyclopedia 99*. CD-ROM.

Parker, Geoffrey. *The Army of Flanders and the Spanish Road, 1567-1659*. Cambridge, England: Cambridge University Press, 1972.

Peters, Ralph. "The Future of Armored Warfare." *Parameters* 27, no. 3 (Autumn 1997): 50-59.

_____. "The Culture of Future Conflict." *Parameters* (Winter 1995): 18-27.

The Population Council. "Population," In *Microsoft Encarta Encyclopedia 99*. CD-ROM.

Preysler, Charles A. "Going Down Town: The Need for Precision MOUT." Fort Leavenworth, KS: U.S. Army School of Advanced Military Studies, monograph, 1995.

Rauch, Jonathon. *The Outnation: A Search for the Soul of Japan*. Boston: Little Brown, 1992.

Ricks, Tom, "Urban Warfare: Where Innovation Hasn't Helped." *Wall Street Journal*, 12 October 1999, 10.

Rosenau, William G. "Every Room Is a New Battle." *Studies in Conflict and Terrorism* 20 (October-December 1997): 371-94.

Rothenberg, Gunther E. "Moltke, Schlieffen, and the Doctrine of Strategic Envelopment." In *Makers of Modern Strategy: From Machiavelli to the*

Nuclear Age. Edited by Peter Paret. Princeton, NJ: Princeton University Press, 1986.

Ryan, Cornelius. *The Last Battle*. New York: Simon and Schuster, 1966.

Sadowski, Yahya M. *The Myth of Global Chaos*. Washington, D. C.: The Brookings Institution, 1998.

Saffold, Timothy L. "The Role of Airpower in Urban Warfare: An Airman's Perspective." *Wright Flyer Paper No. 6*. Maxwell AFB, Alabama: Air Command and Staff College, December 1998.

Scales, Robert H., Jr. "The Indirect Approach: How U. S. Military Forces Can Avoid the Pitfalls of Future Urban Warfare." In *Future Warfare*. Edited by Robert H. Scales. Carlisle Barracks, PA: U. S. Army War College, 1999.

Schmidt, Erich. *Flights over Ancient Cities of Iran*. Chicago, IL: University of Chicago Press, 1940.

Sinnreich, Richard H. "Search of Victory." *Army* (February 1999): 47-50.

Sjoberg, Gideon. *The Preindustrial City: Past and Present*. New York: The Free Press, 1960.

Sun Tzu. *The Art of War*. Translated and with an introduction by Samuel B. Griffith and foreword by B. H. Liddell Hart. Oxford, England: Oxford University Press, 1963.

Tacitus. *The Complete Works of Tacitus*. Translated by Alfred John Church and William Jackson Bodribb and edited, with an introduction, by Moses Hadas. New York: The Modern Library, 1942.

Thomas, Hugh. *The Spanish Civil War*. New York: Harper Colophon Books, 1961.

Thomas, Timothy L. "Air Operations in Low Intensity Conflict: The Case of Chechnya." *Airpower Journal* (Winter 1997): 51-59.

_____. "The Caucasus Conflict and Russian Security: The Russian Armed Forces Confront Chechnya." Fort Leavenworth, KS: Foreign Military Studies Office, 1994.

_____. "The Caucasus Conflict and Russian Security: The Russian Armed Forces Confront Chechnya III. The Battle for Grozny, 1-26 January 1995." *Journal of Slavic Military Studies* 10, no. 1 (March 1997): 50-108.

Thucydides. *History of the Peloponnesian War*. Translated by Rex Warner. London: Penguin Books, 1988.

United Nations. "The World at Six Billion." New York: United Nations Population Division, Department of Economic and Social Affairs, 12 October 1999. At <www.un.org.popin>.

_____. *World Urbanization Prospects: The 1996 Revision, 1997*. At <www.prb.org/pubs, notebook/slide18.jpg>.

United Nations, Department of Economic and Social Affairs, Population Division. "World Urban Agglomerations with Populations of 10 Million or More in 2015." At <www. undoop.org/popin/wdtrends/urb>.

U.S. Army, Headquarters Department of the Army. "Army Demographics, Demographic Profile as of 1 March 1999." Washington, D. C.: Office of the Deputy Chief of Staff for Personnel, Human Resources Directorate, 1999.

U.S. Army, "Urban Combat Operations" *Center for Army Lessons Learned, No. 99-16*, November 1999.

U.S. Army Science Board. *Final Report of the Army Science Board Ad Hoc Group of Military Operations in Built-Up Areas (MOBA)*. Washington, D. C.: Office of the Assistant Secretary of the Army (RDA), January 1979.

U.S. Army Infantry School. "Combat in Cities Report." 3 vols. Fort Benning, GA: U.S. Army Infantry School, 1972.

U.S. Department of Defense. *Report of the Defense Science Board, May, 1986: Conflict Environment Task Force Report: Implications of Third World Environment*. Washington, D. C.: Office of the Undersecretary of Defense for Research and Engineering, May 1986.

U. S. Department of State. *Patterns of Global Terrorism, 1998*. Washington, D. C.: Office of the Coordinator for Counterterrorism, April 1999.

Van Creveld, Martin. *The Sword and the Olive: A Critical History of the Israeli Defense Force*. New York: Public Affairs, 1998.

Van Riper, Paul, and Robert H. Scales. "Preparing for War in the 21st Century." *Parameters* (Autumn 1997): 4-27.

Weber, Eugen. *A Modern History of Europe: Men, Cultures, and Societies from the Renaissance to the Present*. New York: W. W. Norton & Co., 1971.

Weber, Max. *The City.* Translated by Don Martindale and Gertrud Neuwirth. Glencoe, Illinois: The Free Press, 1958.

Weigley, Russell F. *The American Way of War: A History of American Military Strategy and Policy.* New York: Macmillan, 1978.

Weinberg, Gerhard. *A World at Arms: A Global History of World War II.* Cambridge, MA: Cambridge University Press, 1994.

Wijn, J. W. "Military Forces and Warfare." *The New Cambridge Modern History.* Vol. 4. Edited by J. P. Cooper. Cambridge, MA: Cambridge University Press, 1970.

Wyden, Peter. *The Passionate War: The Narrative History of the Spanish Civil War.* New York: Simon and Schuster, 1983.

Ziemke, Earl F. *Stalingrad to Berlin: The German Defeat in the East.* Washington, D. C.: U.S. Army Center of Military History, 1968.

Ziemke, Earl F., and Magna Bauer. *Moscow to Stalingrad: Decision in the East.* Washington, D. C.: U.S. Army Center of Military History, 1987.

No author. "Checking the Interweather." *Time Digital Daily*, 20 December 1999. At <www.pathfinder.com>.

No author. "Chechnya Web Page." At <www.Stud.unihannover.de/~klaasbae/chechnya_html>.

www.ingramcontent.com/pod-product-compliance
Lightning Source LLC
Chambersburg PA
CBHW050501110426
42742CB00018B/3332